Praise for other books in the 101 Inclusive and SEN Lessons *series*

'101 Inclusive and SEN Maths Activities is a brilliant, easy-to-use resource for any teacher. The authors clearly have a profound knowledge and expertise about how children are inspired to learn through having fun! The captivating but simple activities provide the breadth of learning opportunities every child needs.'

— Sue Beaman MBE (for services to special education),
retired headteacher at a special school

'A great resource that busy teachers will dip into again and again. The authors are experienced teachers and provide a no-nonsense fast track to some fantastic tried-and-tested ideas.'

— Adele Devine, special needs teacher, author and co-founder of the
multi-award-winning SEN Assist autism software

'101 Inclusive and SEN Science and Computing Lessons provides teachers with a range of engaging, accessible lessons that highlight the importance of key concept exploration together with the introduction of basic scientific vocabulary. The realistic resource requirement for each lesson highlights how "Supermarket Science" is vital for educational establishments with a limited science budget. The authors have a "real" understanding of how SEN pupils learn by emphasising the importance of visual and kinaesthetic activities. In addition, the lessons are functional, promoting independence and providing our pupils with the opportunity to apply the science they have experienced to "Everyday Life" at home.'

— Julie Neil, special school science consultant and PSQM Gold award winner 2017

'The 101 Inclusive and SEN Lessons series has been an invaluable resource to support inclusion within our school. Each lesson is easy for teachers to implement, yet still manages to be fun and full of opportunities to develop communication and other essential skills.

101 Inclusive and SEN Humanities and Language Lessons is especially useful as this area of the National Curriculum, particularly languages, can seem less accessible for pupils with SEND. With so many ideas to make learning active and concrete, Kate and Claire have again proved that every lesson – and every classroom – can be inclusive.'

— Ashleigh Johnson, autism lead, Netley Primary School and Centre for Autism

T0299705

'As with the other titles in the series *101 Inclusive and SEN Citizenship, PSHE and Religious Education Lessons* provides a fantastically clear, simple and practical resource that can be used by teachers in all settings. Whilst there are specific learning objectives for each activity, the implicit focus of them all is on the development of self-concept and mental wellbeing. That the book covers these vital areas with activities that are fun and engaging is testament to the extensive practical experience Claire and Kate have in walking the talk.'

– Jamie Galpin, developmental psychologist at The Bridge London Trust

101 Inclusive
& SEN Art, Design Technology & Music
Lessons

Also in the 101 Inclusive and SEN Lessons *series*

101 Inclusive and SEN Citizenship, PSHE and Religious Education Lessons
Fun Activities and Lesson Plans for Children Aged 3–11
Claire Brewer and Kate Bradley
ISBN 978 1 78592 368 5
eISBN 978 1 78450 711 4

101 Inclusive and SEN Humanities and Language Lessons
Fun Activities and Lesson Plans for Children Aged 3–11
Kate Bradley and Claire Brewer
ISBN 978 1 78592 367 8
eISBN 978 1 78450 710 7

101 Inclusive and SEN Science and Computing Lessons
Fun Activities and Lesson Plans for Children Aged 3–11
Claire Brewer and Kate Bradley
ISBN 978 1 78592 366 1
eISBN 978 1 78450 709 1

101 Inclusive and SEN English Lessons
Fun Activities and Lesson Plans for Children Aged 3–11
Kate Bradley and Claire Brewer
ISBN 978 1 78592 365 4
eISBN 978 1 78450 708 4

101 Inclusive and SEN Maths Lessons
Fun Activities and Lesson Plans for Children Aged 3–11
Claire Brewer and Kate Bradley
ISBN 978 1 78592 101 8
eISBN 978 1 78450 364 2

101

Inclusive
& SEN Art, Design Technology & Music

Lessons

- - - - - - - - - - -

FUN ACTIVITIES & LESSON PLANS
for Children Aged 3–11

Kate Bradley and Claire Brewer

Jessica Kingsley Publishers
London and Philadelphia

First published in 2020
by Jessica Kingsley Publishers
73 Collier Street
London N1 9BE, UK
and
400 Market Street, Suite 400
Philadelphia, PA 19106, USA

www.jkp.com

Copyright © Kate Bradley and Claire Brewer 2020

Front cover image source: Kara McHale.

All rights reserved. No part of this publication may be reproduced in any material form
(including photocopying, storing in any medium by electronic means or transmitting) without
the written permission of the copyright owner except in accordance with the provisions of
the law or under terms of a licence issued in the UK by the Copyright Licensing Agency
Ltd. www.cla.co.uk or in overseas territories by the relevant reproduction rights organisation,
for details see www.ifrro.org. Applications for the copyright owner's written permission
to reproduce any part of this publication should be addressed to the publisher.

Warning: The doing of an unauthorised act in relation to a copyright work may
result in both a civil claim for damages and criminal prosecution.

Library of Congress Cataloging in Publication Data
A CIP catalog record for this book is available from the Library of Congress

British Library Cataloguing in Publication Data
A CIP catalogue record for this book is available from the British Library

ISBN 978 1 78592 369 2
eISBN 978 1 78450 712 1

Printed and bound in Great Britain by CPI Group (UK) Ltd, Croydon CR0 4YY

Contents

DESIGN AND TECHNOLOGY

MUSIC

DEVELOPING

SECURING

Introduction

Hello and welcome to the sixth book in our '101 Inclusive and SEN Lessons' series!

Whilst changes to school funding are affecting the way schools are able to support complex learners in classrooms, we remain passionate about ensuring children with special educational needs receive a broad, balanced, creative and accessible curriculum. With this book, full of practical and exciting lessons, we hope to support teachers, teaching assistants, parents and other professionals to include all children in their planning and teaching across an increasing range of curriculum subjects.

With the government accepting the recommendations of the Rochford Review and P Levels no longer being a statutory assessment for children working below national curriculum levels from September 2018,[1] we understand that many schools and practitioners may find that there are currently few options to replace them. Thus, we feel that P Levels still offer an invaluable approach to structuring lessons and progression for children with SEN. The lessons in this book are still designed to meet the objectives set out in the P Level document.[2] However, these are simply a guideline to direct adults working with complex learners to choose lessons that are appropriate to the child's current level of understanding and development.

Each chapter starts with lesson objectives designed for the most complex learners and then works up towards more challenging objectives. Plenaries have been included for each lesson in order to provide an obvious end point for the child. We have included ideas for ways to consolidate learning, as for children with SEN, doing an activity once is unlikely to support their understanding of a concept.

The book also includes a chapter of starters designed to engage children in motivating learning styles from the beginning of each lesson. It is up to you to

---

1   Standards and Testing Agency (2016) *Rochford Review: Final Report.* London: DfE.
2   Department for Education & Standards and Testing Agency (2017) *Performance (P Scale) Attainment Targets for Pupils with Special Educational Needs.* London: DfE.

decide which starters suit which lesson you are teaching, as you may want to meet a range of additional skills in one session.

Creativity is such an important part of our lives and for some children it is a skill that needs to be taught to be developed. For many children with SEN the colours, patterns and freedom to explore that can be offered through subjects such as Art and Design and Music can really open up whole new worlds of learning and experience. Design Technology offers the chance to develop core skills such as planning and executing an idea and understanding the impact that building and design can have on our environment. Above all, these creative subjects can be truly inclusive as they can be taught through visual, tactile and auditory experiences which can really appeal to the strengths of children with SEN.

We have both used many of these ideas in our classrooms and wider practice and hope that you enjoy teaching with them in yours!

Best wishes

Kate and Claire

Follow and share your ideas with us: @Kate_Brads, @clairebrewers

What Do We Mean by Additional Skills?

- Kinaesthetic: movement is important to stimulate the child and provide learning experiences that do not revolve around sitting at a table and chair.

- Auditory: being able to develop listening and processing skills in a variety of subjects across the school day will support children to become more attentive in lessons and life.

- Fine motor: these are the skills that involve doing activities on a smaller scale. Developing these skills supports handwriting, dressing and manipulation in the long term.

- Gross motor: these involve the big muscle groups in the body and are large-scale movements. Developing these skills supports trunk control, coordination and motor planning.

- Tactile: skin covers the entirety of the body and is the largest sensory system. Having difficulties processing tactile input (such as getting messy) means that the children don't explore and experience the world to its full potential.

- Attention: a child's ability to attain and engage in activities to their full extent needs time and patience. The ability to focus on an individual activity for a longer period of time enables learning to take place. By providing exciting, short activities you can build a child's tolerance to this.

- Communication: with reference to communication, this is about receptive (listening to) and expressive (responding to) language. Language does not have to be speech; this can be in the form of visuals, switches and gesture.

- Social communication: this is about the vital skills of sharing time and experience with a partner, turn taking and knowing rules within social situations and games.

Resources

This is not an exhaustive list but, where possible, we have used resources that we find easily in our own classrooms so that life is not made harder for you by having to go out of your way to prepare extra resources for the lessons.

Resources that you will use throughout the book:

- builder's tray

- choosing board (large firm board with strips of Velcro to attach symbols and pictures)

- laminating sheets and access to a laminator

- water and sand tray

- range of paint colours

- paint trays

- paintbrushes

- PVA glue

- glue spreaders

- glue sticks

- coloured card

- scissors

- specialist scissors (recommended by an occupational therapist if necessary)

- range of material and fabric

- sewing materials

- paper

- aprons

- tape (masking and sticky)

- cooking equipment

- lollipop sticks

- interactive whiteboard (IWB)

- whiteboard and pens

- chalks

- pastels

- charcoal

- clay

- tools for working with clay

- play dough

- tools for working with play dough

- crayons

- range of musical instruments

- sound boards

- CD player/speakers

- electronic tablet

- camera

- large pocket dice

- sketchbooks

- junk modelling resources (cardboard rolls, egg cartons, plastic and cardboard boxes, yoghurt pots, etc.).

STARTERS

Diagonal Dance

RESOURCES

None

ACTIVITY

- Support the children to lie on the floor or sit on a chair.

- Demonstrate bringing together opposite arm and foot, singing 'This is the way we touch our toes, touch our toes, touch our toes'. Keep doing the movement and sing 'This is the way we squeeze our toes...'.

- Support the children to take part in the song.

Colour Spot

RESOURCES

Large pocket dice with different colour symbols in each pocket

A4 laminated colour symbols to match those on the dice

ACTIVITY

- Support a group of three to four children to come to the front of the class/group.

- Choose a child to roll the dice and then name the colour it lands on.

- The other children in the group race to the correct colour symbol.

- The last child to reach the correct colour spot is out and the activity is repeated until there is a winner.

Shape Maker

RESOURCES

Two simple shape symbols in a large pocket dice, e.g. square and triangle

Pieces of card cut into lengths that will make the shapes

ACTIVITY

- Ask two children to come to the front of the class/group.

- One child rolls the dice and identifies the shape.

- The children then work together to use the lengths of card to make the shape on the floor.

Syllable Sounds

RESOURCES

A drum or tambourine

ACTIVITY

- Support the children to sit in a semicircle.

- Choose a child and model saying their name and banging the drum or tambourine to the number of syllables in their name, e.g. if name is 'Annabelle' bang the drum for each syllable: 'Ann' 'a' 'belle'.

- Then go around the group and support each child to bang the drum, saying their name and hitting the drum for each syllable of their name.

Paint Me Here

RESOURCES

Large white paper

Easel

Bull clips

Range of paint colours

Colour symbols to match paint

Paintbrushes

ACTIVITY

- To set up this starter attach the large white paper to the easel using the bull clips and place the paint next to the easel.

- Support the children to sit in a semicircle facing the easel.

- Ask each child to come up to the easel, choose a paint colour from the symbols and then use the paint and paintbrush to mark make on the white paper on the easel to self-register.

- If the children are able, support them to paint the first letter of their name or a self-portrait.

Bounce, Bounce

RESOURCES

Large white paper

Aprons

Bouncy ball for each child

Paint

ACTIVITY

- Place the large piece of paper on the floor (outside may be better!) and ask everyone to wear an apron. Give each child a bouncy ball.

- Everyone rolls the bouncy ball in paint and, on three, everyone drops their ball on the paper.

- Retrieve the balls and repeat.

All Together Now

RESOURCES

Large piece of white paper

Pens, pencils, crayons, paint and paintbrush and highlighter for each child

Large pocket dice with pen, pencil, crayon, paint and highlighter images

ACTIVITY

- Everyone sits around the table with a large piece of paper in the middle.

- Each child should have a pen, pencil, crayon, paintbrush and paint and highlighters.

- Roll the dice; note the image that it lands on: everyone needs to use that tool to add marks to the paper.

- Repeat.

Replicate

RESOURCES

Picture of famous painting

Paper

Crayons

Timer

ACTIVITY

- Show the children a famous painting, giving them 3 minutes to try and re-create this. Encourage them to look at the colours and shapes.

- Model doing this first, and then start the timer for the children.

Technique

RESOURCES

Paper split into four squares

Sharp pencils

ACTIVITY

- Everyone sits around a table with a piece of paper and a pencil.

- Model shading as a technique in the first square; children copy.

- Model cross-hatching in the second square; children copy.

- Model using dots close together and further apart in the third square; children copy.

- In the final square, children can practise their favourite technique.

Stitch It

RESOURCES

Small piece of Binca fabric for each child

Needle

Thread

ACTIVITY

• Provide the children with the fabric, needle and thread.

• See if they can thread the needle; if not, help them with this.

• Model making a stitch.

• Closely supervise each child while they stitch.

ART

1. Sunflower Strokes

Learning Objective

Emerging

Pupils are aware of starting or stopping a process.

Additional Skills

Gross motor: using core to support self on the floor.

Fine motor: using a grip on the pastels to make marks.

Auditory: stopping and starting an activity following an auditory cue.

Resources

Large sheets of paper

Masking tape

Pastels in yellows, oranges and greens

Large copies of Van Gogh's painting *Sunflowers*

Music to paint to, such as Vivaldi's *Four Seasons*

MAIN

- To set up this activity, tape the large paper to the floor and place the pastels around the paper.

- Support the children to come and sit on the floor by the paper in a space next to the pastels.

- Show the children Van Gogh's pictures and identify the colours and features.

- Place a vase of real sunflowers in the middle of the large paper and explain that today we are going to make our own sunflower pictures.

- We will start when the music starts and stop when the music stops.

- Play the music and support children to make marks using the pastels, briefly looking at the sunflowers for inspiration.

- Periodically stop the music and everyone stops drawing. Encourage children to look at drawing and look at sunflower to review drawing.

- Start the music again and everyone starts drawing again.

- Continue for as long as children can maintain attention.

PLENARY

Stop the music for a final time and count down '5, 4, 3, 2, 1, painting has finished.' Support the children to stand up and look at their drawings; do they look like Van Gogh's?

CONSOLIDATION ACTIVITIES

Use music as an auditory cue to start and stop other activities across the day, e.g. play music to prompt the children to come and sit in the circle, play music at the end of playtime to signal the end of the play.

2. Firework Fingers

Learning Objective

Emerging

Pupils make marks intentionally on a surface with fingers or tools.

Additional Skills

Fine motor: using one finger to make marks.

Auditory: making marks in response to music.

Tactile: experiencing and tolerating sensory media such as paint.

Resources

Large white paper

Tape

Different coloured paints in different pots

Access to firework images and music (e.g. a clip of the London New Year's Eve fireworks on the interactive whiteboard)

MAIN

- To set up this activity, tape the large paper to a table top and place the pots of different coloured paint along the paper.

- Support the children to come and sit in a semicircle ready to learn.

- Show the children the images and music of fireworks and identify the colours, supporting the children to track the movement of the fireworks.

- Support the children to come to the table and model placing a finger in a pot of paint, naming the colour and then making a 'whoosh' sound while making a swishing mark on the paper in imitation of a firework.

- Support the children to choose a colour, place their finger in the paint and make swishing movements to make marks that imitate fireworks.

- Play the firework music and images in the background whilst the children are painting.

PLENARY

Support the children to use their finger, paintbrush or pen to 'sign' their work alongside the marks they have made.

CONSOLIDATION ACTIVITIES

Repeat this activity using different sensory media and tools, e.g. using paintbrushes, dipping dishcloths in paint and throwing them at the paper.

3. Brilliant Butterflies

Learning Objective

Emerging

Pupils repeat an activity to make the same or similar effect.

Additional Skills

Visual: beginning to recognise similarities in patterns.

Fine motor: using pinching motion to fold paper.

Communication: making a choice from two colours.

Resources

Pictures of butterflies

White paper

Symbols to match the colours of paints available

Different coloured paints in different pots

Paintbrushes

Large piece of white paper

MAIN

- Support the children to come and sit in a semicircle ready to learn.

- Sit in front of the group and name all the resources.

- Show the pictures of butterflies and point out how the patterns are the same on both sides.

- Model folding the white paper and opening it up again, choosing a colour symbol, matching it to the correct paint colour and making a pattern on one side of the paper, folding the paper again and then opening it to reveal the symmetrical pattern.

- Support children to move to the table to take part in the activity as independently as possible.

- Encourage the children to repeat this activity several times to make several butterflies.

PLENARY

Support the children to come back to the semicircle where the lesson began. Support each child to come to the front, choose a colour, make a shape on one side of the large piece of white paper and then all together fold the paper and open it again to reveal a giant butterfly.

CONSOLIDATION ACTIVITIES

Set this activity up in the outside space with the pictures of butterflies available and encourage the children to be as independent as possible in creating similar effects with the resources.

4. Roll-a-Mark

Learning Objective

Emerging

Pupils begin to carry out simple processes.

Additional Skills

Gross motor: handling different sized balls.

Tactile: experiencing different textures and sensory media.

Visual: watching the consequences of actions.

Resources

Large white paper

Builder's tray

Different coloured paints

Paint trays

Different textured balls (e.g. bobbly balls, spiky balls, etc.)

Box

Pen or pencil

MAIN

• To set up this activity tape the large white paper to the bottom of the builder's tray. Pour the different coloured paints onto separate trays and place them next to the builder's tray. Place the textured balls into the box and place the box next to the builder's tray.

• Support the child to come over to the builder's tray. Model finding a ball in the box, feeling it and labelling the texture, e.g. 'bumpy', 'smooth', etc.

• Model rolling the ball in paint and then pushing the ball around the white paper on the builder's tray to make marks.

• Support the child to complete the process as independently as possible: pulling a ball out of the box, exploring the ball, placing it in paint and then pushing it around to make marks.

• Repeat this using different coloured paints until the child has explored all the balls.

PLENARY

Support the child to look at the artwork they have created and to use a pen or pencil to 'sign' their work. Then support the child to find a place in the classroom to pin up their artwork for display.

CONSOLIDATION ACTIVITIES

Repeat this activity and process with different sensory items in the box, e.g. different textured materials such as dishcloth, sponge, etc., fruit and vegetables such as potato, avocado, etc.

5. Creative Carousel

Learning Objective

Emerging

Pupils choose tools and materials appropriate to the activity.

Additional Skills

Attention: transitioning from one activity to another when directed.

Fine motor: using a palmer grip to use different mark making tools.

Visual: watching the marks made by different sensory media.

Resources

Different coloured chalks

Chalkboards

Different coloured whiteboard pens

Whiteboards

Different coloured paints

Paintbrushes

White paper

Symbols for 'chalk', 'pen', 'paintbrush'

MAIN

- To set up this activity place the coloured chalks and chalkboards on one table, the whiteboard pens and whiteboards on a second table and the paintbrushes, paints and paper on a third table. Place the relevant symbol with each material.

- Support a small group of children to sit at each table and encourage them to explore the tools and materials using simple language to label the tools and materials, e.g. 'You are using chalk on the chalkboard.'

- After a few minutes of exploring and using the tools and materials at one table, count down '5, 4, 3, 2, 1, time to move to next table.'

- Support the children to move to the next table to explore the tools and materials there.

- Repeat this until all the children have explored the three tables.

PLENARY

Support the children to come and sit in a semicircle and place a chalkboard, whiteboard and paper with a pot of paint on the floor in front of the group. Choose a child and give them an art material, e.g. pen, chalk or paintbrush, and ask them to match it to the correct item on the floor. Allow every child to take a turn.

CONSOLIDATION ACTIVITIES

Repeat the creative carousel across several weeks and slowly introduce different materials and tools, e.g. clay and sculpting tools, play dough and play dough tools, etc. Each time conclude the lesson with the children matching the tools to the correct activity.

6. And Again

Learning Objective

Emerging

Pupils repeat an activity to make the same or similar effect.

Additional Skills

Visual: making marks on the page.

Fine motor: using tools to make marks.

Social interaction: working alongside others.

Resources

Different coloured paints

Paint trays

Paintbrush

Roller

Little mop

Sponge

Paper

Aprons

MAIN

- Place out three colours of paint and add a paintbrush, roller, little mop and sponge in each colour.

- Place strips of paper at each child's place.

- When the children arrive for the lesson, support them to put on an apron. Model choosing two different tools from the paint trays and make alternate marks on the paper, naming as they go, e.g. 'blue paintbrush, yellow sponge, blue paintbrush, yellow sponge'.

- Encourage children to repeat the activity; they may want to use a range of colours and tools and this is fine. Encourage the children to be creative.

PLENARY

When the children have finished, support them to put their work to dry and to go and wash the paint and tools. Count down '5, 4, 3, 2, 1, finished' and end the session.

CONSOLIDATION ACTIVITIES

On an easel in the room, place strips of paper vertically and offer one colour of paint with two painting tools to encourage the children to repeat actions or make patterns.

7. Bringing the World Inside

Learning Objective

Emerging

Pupils explore materials systematically.

Additional Skills

Tactile: choosing materials that have similar properties.

Fine motor: using tools appropriately.

Social interaction: working alongside others.

Resources

Bag for each child

Aprons

Tree outline on paper

PVA glue

Paintbrush

MAIN

- Link this activity to a current theme or topic; this example is going to use autumn.

- Before the lesson take the children out on a nature walk (follow appropriate setting guidelines and risk assessments); give each child a bag and tell them they are looking for materials to use in art to make a picture. Encourage the children to collect leaves, bark and sticks.

- When back in class, each child should put on an apron. Give each child the template of a tree.

- Place all the items that were collected on to the table, and group them (all leaves together, all bark together, etc.).

- Provide the children with PVA glue and a paintbrush and encourage them to choose items and stick them down to make a tree.

PLENARY

Once everyone has finished, ask the children to help by placing their art to dry and wiping the tables.

CONSOLIDATION ACTIVITIES

Place the leftover natural materials in a builder's tray and add some small world people so that the children can explore the textures and items in a free choice activity.

8. Keep to the Line

Learning Objective

Emerging

Pupils are aware of starting or stopping a process.

Additional Skills

Visual: making marks on the page.

Fine motor: using tools to make marks.

Social interaction: working alongside others.

Auditory: listening to 'start' and 'stop'.

Resources

Yogurt pots

Different coloured paints

Lollipop sticks

Access to a freezer

Large white paper

Marker pens

Tape

Aprons

MAIN

- The night before the lesson, prepare mixtures of watered-down paint in a variety of colours. Place these in yogurt pots with a lolly stick and put in the freezer overnight.

- Place a large sheet of paper on the floor and with a marker pen; make a variety of lines (squiggles, straight, zigzags) along the length of the paper. Place aprons around the paper ready for the children to use. Take the yogurt pots from the freezer and loosen the sticks so that they are easy to pull out.

- Invite the children to come and join you. Help the children roll their sleeves and put on their aprons.

- Hand each child a paint stick and model to them starting at one end and making a paint line along the paper.

- Encourage the children to swap the colours of paint they are using. Use the language 'start' and 'stop' when the children are working across the lines.

PLENARY

If all the lines have been completed, hand a marker pen to a child and ask them to make a line that they can then go over the top. Once the paper is full, count down '5, 4, 3, 2, 1, finished'. Help the children to tidy and wash their hands.

CONSOLIDATION ACTIVITIES

In fine motor activities, place lines on paper and encourage the children to rip or cut along the lines to practise the start and stop within the process.

9. Paint Bags

Learning Objective

Emerging

Pupils make marks intentionally on a surface with fingers or tools.

Additional Skills

Fine motor: making marks in paint/on bag.

Visual: copying an adult.

Social communication: working alongside others.

Resources

Aprons

Different coloured paints

Glitter

Tray

Ziplock bags

Electrical tape

MAIN

- Help all the children to put on aprons. Place the selection of paint and glitter in a tray in front of the group.

- Model choosing a paint colour and squeezing some into the ziplock bag and then shaking in some glitter.

- All children take a turn at adding paint and glitter.

- Once all the bags are made, stick them with electrical tape to the window.

- Encourage the children to make marks so that they can see the light shining through. These could be shapes or letters of the alphabet, for example.

PLENARY

Count down '5, 4, 3, 2, 1, finished'. Help the children to tidy up.

CONSOLIDATION ACTIVITIES

Leave the bags on the window. Each day add a different picture or shape next to the paint bags and encourage the children to copy this.

10. Peg Painting

Learning Objective

Emerging

Pupils show some awareness of cause and effect in a creative process.

Additional Skills

Visual: making marks on the page.

Fine motor: using tools to make marks.

Social communication: working alongside others.

Resources

Pegs

Cotton wool balls

Paint trays

Different coloured paints

White paper

Sellotape

Aprons

MAIN

- Set up the activity by pegging a piece of cotton wool to each peg. Fill up paint trays with brightly coloured paint. Lay the white paper on the table and tape this down, and put out an apron for each child.

- Invite the children to the group; help them to roll up their sleeves and put on their apron.

- Model using the peg like a paintbrush and make marks on the paper.

- Encourage the children to join in.

PLENARY

Write the child's name next to the marks that they have made and help the children to wash their hands once the activity has finished.

CONSOLIDATION ACTIVITIES

Use other non-typical items to paint with, such as washing up brushes, forks, etc., to allow the children to explore making marks in a variety of ways.

11. The Creature

Learning Objective

Emerging

Pupils show an active interest in a range of tools and materials.

Additional Skills

Visual: selecting preferred materials.

Fine motor: using tools to make marks in 3D objects.

Social communication: working alongside others, sharing resources.

Resources

Play dough or clay

Tools (scissors, pencils, wooden knives, etc.)

Art materials (pipe cleaner, sequins, foam shapes, tissue paper, etc.)

Bowls

Squares of card

Marker pens

MAIN

- Place the play dough or clay in a bowl in the middle of the table. In cups or bowls around it place the tools, sequins, googly eyes, tissue paper, foam shapes, etc.

- Place pictures of animals and aliens around the bowls for inspiration.

- Sitting or working as a group, adults and children all take a piece of play dough or clay and begin making a creature.

- Adults hand the children items or offer the bowl if they are not taking too much interest.

PLENARY

Everyone should place their creature on a card and mark make or write their name on it and leave it out to dry. All help tidy the activity.

CONSOLIDATION ACTIVITIES

Look at each others' models and think about what they could be called or where they might live. Offer the activity again with different resources and see if the children can make a creature friend.

12. Dip Dip

Learning Objective

Emerging

Pupils show they can create and apply familiar techniques to a task.

Additional Skills

Fine motor: using one finger.

Social communication: working alongside others, sharing resources.

Attention: working for 7–10 minutes.

Resources

Aprons

Large paper

Paint in small containers

MAIN

• Create an outline of a character from a book that you are currently studying on a large piece of paper. Place this on a large table along with a picture of the character so that the children can identify the colours.

• Provide each child with an apron.

• Place small containers of paint in appropriate colours around the character.

• Model looking at the picture and naming a colour. Find the correct paint and dip first finger into the paint. Find the part of the character that matches the picture and begin dabbing finger in that area.

• Support the children to do the same.

Teaching note: if a child does not like to get messy, allow them to use a small paintbrush.

PLENARY

Once everyone has spent time completing the character, ask the children to go and wash their hands and count down the activity to finish.

CONSOLIDATION ACTIVITIES

On the playground on a sunny day, draw around the outline of one of the children in chalk. Provide small containers of water and encourage the children to 'finger paint' with the water.

13. Please Can I Have

Learning Objective

Emerging

Pupils choose tools or materials that are appropriate to the activity.

Additional Skills

Fine motor: using a range of tools.

Social communication: working alongside others, sharing resources.

Kinaesthetic: moving between activities.

Communication: using a sentence to request an item.

Resources

Large white paper

Tape

Aprons

Three pots of different coloured paint

Tools, e.g. paintbrushes, plastic cutlery, hairbrushes, paint rollers

Visual symbols of each of the pieces of equipment

MAIN

- Place tables together to form a shared workspace. Cover this with large sheets of paper and tape to the table. Do not place any of the art materials on the table; this activity is going to encourage the children to communicate for what they need.

- When the children join the activity, support them to put on an apron. One adult sits to the left of the table and shows the children the paints; another adult (if available) sits to the right of the table with a range of tools. Make it clear to the children that the adults have these items.

- Hand the children the set of visuals and support them to make the sentence 'adult x I want item x'; this could read 'Kate I want paintbrush' or 'Claire I want red paint'.

- Children take their visual sentence to the appropriate adult and request the items that they need to paint with.

- Children then have time to paint with the items that they have requested.

PLENARY

At the end of the session, write the name of the child on the work and leave it to dry. Encourage the children to begin to help tidy up.

CONSOLIDATION ACTIVITIES

The visual sentence supports can be used for a range of classroom activities, such as snacks or PE. Change the items to the items available for the session and the same visuals can be re-used.

14. Spray It!

Learning Objective

Emerging

Pupils handle or use tools and materials purposefully.

Additional Skills

Visual: noticing colours mixing.

Fine motor: squeezing the handle of the spray bottle.

Social communication: working alongside others, sharing resources.

Resources

Spray bottles

Different coloured paints

White paper

Newspaper

Aprons

MAIN

• Fill the spray bottles with slightly watered-down paint and label the bottles so that the children can see what colour is inside. Stick large white paper along a wall or cupboard side. Place newspaper along the floor to catch the drips.

• Invite the children to the space; ask them to put on an apron. Model to the children choosing a colour, pointing the spray bottle at the paper and squeezing the handle. Watch the paint run down the paper.

• Hand each child a spray bottle and direct them to spray at the paper.

• Encourage the children to change colours and see what happens when they get mixed.

PLENARY

All spray bottles should be placed on the side; count down '5, 4, 3, 2, 1, finished'. Leave the paper to dry and then help to wash the children's hands.

CONSOLIDATION ACTIVITIES

Carry out this activity again. On the paper place shapes and templates that relate to your topic. When the paint is dry, move the shapes with the children so that you can reveal the shapes underneath.

15. The One I Choose

Learning Objective

Emerging

Pupils show preferences for activities and begin to carry out simple processes.

Additional Skills

Fine motor: using a range of tools.

Social communication: working alongside others, sharing resources.

Kinaesthetic: moving between activities.

Resources

Bowls

Coloured tissue paper

A4 white paper

PVA glue

Glue spreaders

Different coloured paints

Paint trays

Sponge or potatoes to cut into shapes for printing

Large paper

Aprons

MAIN

• Set up two tables, each with a different art activity. On the first table place bowls of coloured paper squares, A4 white paper with the outline of an animal (or something linked to your topic), PVA glue and glue spreaders. On the second table place out two trays of paint (in two different colours) and some sponges or potatoes cut in to animal shapes (or something linked to your topic). Cover the second table with paper.

• When the children arrive, help them to put on an apron. Model both of the activities and allow the child to choose which one they want to participate in.

• Let them swap between the two, so that they have a chance at both, and see which one they show more of a preference for.

PLENARY

At the end of the session, write the name of the child on the work or next to their prints and leave these to dry. Encourage the children to begin to help tidy up.

CONSOLIDATION ACTIVITIES

Place out two art easels; on one of them place crayons and repeating patterns and the other large shapes and paints. Allow the children to explore both and see what their preference is.

16. Geo Art

Learning Objective

Developing

Pupils start to use tools to produce a piece of work.

Additional Skills

Fine motor: using a range of tools.

Social communication: working alongside others, sharing resources.

Attention: working for 10–15 minutes.

Visual: noticing patterns.

Resources

Aprons

Three square pieces of card for each child (make sure masking tape can peel off without damaging)

Masking tape

Different coloured paints

Paintbrushes

MAIN

• Give each child in the group an apron.

• Place the first piece of card in front of each child. Adult also takes a card.

• Model using the masking tape to place strips of tape at different angles across the card (about seven to ten in total).

• Give each child time to do this for themselves. Support only once the child has tried themselves.

• Once everyone has done this, give each child two more pieces of card and encourage them to repeat the task of sticking masking tape across the card.

• Once everyone has finished, pack the masking tape away.

• Model using paint to colour a section of the card, then choose another colour for another section. Talk about working slowly and neatly.

• Children should be given time to paint their three boards.

PLENARY

Children mark initials on their work and place them on the drying rack. Everyone helps tidy up.

CONSOLIDATION ACTIVITIES

Once the work has dried, come back together as a group. Slowly peel off the masking tape from the adult's piece and show the children the art that has been created. Support the children to do the same. Encourage the children to place them in an order they like, and stick them to a larger piece of card. Show the children work by modern geometric artists and talk about similarities in their own work.

17. Leaf Garland

Learning Objective

Developing

Pupils practise new skills with less support.

Additional Skills

Fine motor: using a needle and thread.

Social communication: working alongside others, sharing resources.

Attention: working for 10–15 minutes.

Visual: noticing patterns.

Resources

Leaves

Twine

Plastic needles

Scissors

MAIN

- In the outdoor area, pre-make some garlands out of leaves threaded onto twine.

- On a table, place plastic needles for threading, scissors, twine and a selection of leaves.

- Write the instructions down with visuals so that the children can access these.

- Invite the children to the activity. Point out the pre-made hanging garlands.

- Leave the children to start the activity. Only offer support when they seek assistance (threading the needle, for example). Where possible try and model and teach the skill so that the child can attempt it themselves, rather than the adults doing it for them.

PLENARY

Once everyone has made a garland, help the children to hang these around the outdoor area.

CONSOLIDATION ACTIVITIES

Take the children on a scavenger hunt for materials that they can do outdoor craft with.

18. SSSSSSnake

Learning Objective

Developing

Pupils show an intention to create.

Additional Skills

Fine motor: using a range of tools.

Social communication: working alongside others, sharing resources.

Attention: working for 7–10 minutes.

Resources

Aprons

Paper plates

Paint in small containers

Scrap paper

Crayons

Glue and spreaders

Scissors

MAIN

• Provide each child with an apron and a paper plate.

• Put out a range of resources such as paints, crayons, scrap paper and glue.

• Allow the children time to work with the different material to decorate their plates.

• Put the plates to one side to dry.

PLENARY

Everyone should wash hands and help tidy up. Come back together as a group and, providing that the plate is dry enough to handle, model cutting a curve from the outside to the inside of the plate (to make a snake). Be really excited about showing the children what has been made. Support the children to cut their plates to make their own snakes.

CONSOLIDATION ACTIVITIES

When the snake plates are completely dry, attach a piece of string to one end and hang these from the ceiling or another suitable space. Encourage the children to look at the work they have created.

19. Whose Footprints?

Learning Objective

Developing

Pupils show an intention to create.

Additional Skills

Tactile: experiencing sensory media on the skin.

Fine motor: taking shoes and socks off.

Visual: awareness of making marks using body parts.

Communication: indicating choice using symbol/gesture/speech.

Resources

Large and long roll of paper or large white sheet

Masking tape

Washing up bowls with water

Towels

A range of paint colours

Flat trays

Colour symbols to match paint colours

Camera/electronic tablet

MAIN

- To set up this activity, tape the large paper/sheet securely to the floor. Line up enough chairs for each child in the small group alongside the paper/sheet. Have the washing up bowls with water and towels to hand. Squeeze each paint colour onto a separate tray.

- Support the children to come and sit on the chairs and take off shoes and socks as independently as possible. Place socks and shoes under the table.

- Model choosing a paint colour from the colour symbols and, whilst sat down, placing their bare feet in the paint then walking along the paper/sheet looking at the marks they are making.

- Then support each child to choose a paint colour; place their bare feet in the paint tray and make footprint marks on the paper/sheet.

- When the child has finished, support them to sit back down, wash their feet with the water and towels and put shoes and socks back on. Draw their attention back to the paper/sheet to look at footprints.

PLENARY

Once the artwork is dry show the finished piece to the children, along with photos of them taking part in the creative activity. Support each child to identify their footprints and mark make alongside one of their footprints, using a pen to sign their work.

CONSOLIDATION ACTIVITIES

The finished piece could be used as a display/backing for a display. Draw the child's attention to it so that they notice the results of their creative actions.

20. Collage à Toi

Learning Objective

Developing

Pupils start to use tools, materials and simple actions to produce a piece of work.

Additional Skills

Fine motor: beginning to use scissors.

Visual: using different shapes to create patterns.

Attention: maintaining attention for up to 10 minutes to complete a task.

Social communication: identifying a friend or another child in the group to use for their artwork.

Resources

Colour photocopies of pictures of the children in the group

Different coloured card

Scissors (specialist scissors recommended by an occupational therapist may be necessary)

Glue sticks

MAIN

- Support the children to come and sit in a semicircle ready to learn.

- On the floor in front of the group, model looking at the colour photocopies of the children's faces and choosing a friend's photo to use for their artwork.

- Model choosing a piece of coloured card, taking the scissors and cutting a shape and sticking it onto the coloured photocopy using the glue stick. Repeat several times until the coloured photocopy face has become a collage of coloured card shapes.

- Then tell the group it is their turn.

- Support the children to transition to the table. Support the children to choose the photocopy of a friend to use in their artwork.

- Support the children to cut up the card using scissors and to make a collage of their friends' faces.

PLENARY

Support the children to come back to the semicircle with their artwork. Support each child to come to the front with their artwork and ask the child who is in the photocopy to come and stand next to the artwork. Take a photo for comparison. Repeat this for all the children.

CONSOLIDATION ACTIVITIES

During free time activities and other lessons support the child to use scissors and glue with increasing independence.

21. Tile It

Learning Objective

Developing

Pupils start to use tools to produce a piece of work.

Additional Skills

Fine motor: using a range of tools.

Social communication: working alongside others, sharing resources.

Attention: working for 10–15 minutes.

Visual: noticing patterns.

Resources

Aprons

Paper

Pencils

Rulers

Clay pre-prepared in squares (the size of a tile)

Plastic clay tools

MAIN

- Give each child in the group an apron.

- On paper, encourage each of the children to draw out a pattern; encourage zigzags, circles, diagonal lines, etc. Provide rulers if you think this will support them to make the patterns.

- Ask each child to review their work; are they happy with their pattern? If not, take another turn.

- Place the squares of clay in front of each child; tell them they need to copy their pattern on to the clay. Show the children how to safely use the plastic tools to score clay.

- Give the children around 5–8 minutes to work on this; watch carefully so that they do not cut all the way through.

PLENARY

Ask each child to make their initials somewhere on their clay square and to place it on a large board to dry. Then ask the children to help tidy up.

CONSOLIDATION ACTIVITIES

Once the clay squares have dried, provide paint so that the children can make their pieces colourful. Once the paint has dried, find a place where the squares can be displayed, perhaps in the school garden.

22. Design Me Part 1

Learning Objective

Developing

Pupils purposefully choose techniques.

Additional Skills

Social communication: talking about ideas.

Attention: working for 15–20 minutes.

Fine motor: using a pencil.

Resources

A4 paper with design template (what object are you going to make, what materials are you going to use, how are you going to stick it together?, etc.)

Pencils

MAIN

- Give each child a piece of A4 paper with 'design template' outline.

- Model completing one, talking through their process.

- Children should be given time to plan their model. Encourage them to think about resources that are available in the classroom.

- Make suggestions if necessary, or ask questions such as 'What colours could you use?' 'Is paper stronger than card?', etc.

PLENARY

Once everyone has finished, share each of the designs with the rest of the group. Encourage the children to talk about their design and how they are going to make it.

CONSOLIDATION ACTIVITIES

Spend time with each child gathering the resources that they will need ready for the Part 2 lesson.

23. Design Me Part 2

Learning Objective

Developing

Pupils work in 3D to represent an object.

Additional Skills

Social communication: asking and answering questions.

Attention: working for 15–20 minutes.

Fine motor: using a range of tools.

Resources

Design template from 'Design Me Part 1'

Resources for each child's work from 'Design Me Part 1'

Scissors

Glue

String

MAIN

- Hand out the design template from the Part 1 lesson. Give each child time to look at them. Is everyone happy with what they are going to make, or does anyone want to make a change?

- Present each child with the resources that they collected with the adult previously so that they are ready to make their model.

- Encourage each child to go and find the classroom equipment they need (scissors, glue, string, etc.).

- Work alongside the children to make the models and encourage them to refer to their design template to look at the colours and shapes they originally chose.

PLENARY

At the end of the lesson, ask each child to safely place their model in the allocated space and then tidy up their resources.

CONSOLIDATION ACTIVITIES

The following day (or when the models are dry) ask each child to present their design template and model to the group. Others in the group can ask questions that the child can then answer about their work.

24. Sew Time

Learning Objective

Developing

Pupils show confidence in using a variety of tools and materials.

Additional Skills

Social communication: sharing an experience.

Attention: working for 15–20 minutes.

Fine motor: using a needle and thread.

Visual: noticing what an adult has modelled.

Resources

Needles

Coloured thread

Squares of fabric (something firm is best)

MAIN

- Everyone sits around a table. Model to the group choosing a thread and threading a needle.

- Each child repeats this process so that everyone has a coloured thread on a needle.

- Model choosing a square of fabric and making a stitch through this, being careful of the fingers. Repeat this a few times so that a pattern emerges.

- Support the children with their first stitch hand over hand so that they can feel what this is like, then step away and encourage the children to take a turn by themselves.

- Children can change coloured thread if they wish; support where necessary.

PLENARY

After 20 minutes, stop the session. Ask everyone to finish their last stitch and to make a knot so that the thread does not come loose. If the children are happy with their sewing, then it can be put in the finished box; if they want to spend more time on it, place it in the sewing box.

CONSOLIDATION ACTIVITIES

Repeat this lesson a few times over the course of a week or half term. Once everyone has made a few squares, these can be sewn together and backed to make a blanket or rug that the children can then use in their book corner.

25. Shake Me Up!

Learning Objective

Developing

Pupils communicate their ideas through their use of colour.

Additional Skills

Social communication: working alongside others, sharing resources.

Attention: working for 15–20 minutes.

Visual: selecting items of the same colour.

Resources

Range of items for bottle (glitter, sequins, small world characters, beads, jewels, etc.)

Trays

Range of food colouring

Clean plastic bottles

Jug

MAIN

- Place a range of materials into trays on the table; ensure that they are sorted by colour.

- Invite the children to join the group.

- Explain that everyone is going to make a sensory bottle, and that they can choose extra special items to put into it.

- Model choosing a colour, and then using available resources to place in bottle. Ask the children to help the adult look in the room for other items that can be included. Talk about why paper and similar materials are not suitable when mixed with water.

- Add food colouring of the chosen colour to a jug and water.

- Pour this into the bottle. Close the lid tightly and give the bottle a shake.

- Give each child a bottle and support them to choose a colour for the items and then explore the room for more.

PLENARY

Once everyone has finished, sit in a group and pass the bottles around so that everyone can take a turn at looking at the patterns and colours.

CONSOLIDATION ACTIVITIES

Place the sensory bottles in a calm box so that the children can access these through the day.

26. Im-press Me! Part 1

Learning Objective

Developing

Pupils practise new skills with less support, developing their knowledge of the process of making.

Additional Skills

Kinaesthetic: moving around in new environments.

Fine motor: using a pincer grip to select foliage.

Attention: recalling a process and activity from a previous day or week.

Resources

Large copies of Monet's painting *Water Lilies*

Colour bingo board to match the colours found in the painting

PVA glue

Glue spreaders

MAIN

• Support children to sit in a semicircle ready to learn.

• Show the group the image of Claude Monet's *Water Lilies* and encourage the children to identify the colours they can see.

• Explain that we are going to go outside and find plants and flowers to match the colours found in the painting.

• Support the children to take a colour bingo board and explore an outside area, finding flowers, plants and leaves, etc. that match the colours on the bingo board, and support the children to take a sample of each plant/flower/leaf that they find.

• Once back in the classroom, support the children to match their samples of plants/flowers/leaves to the large copies of the painting and use the glue spreaders and glue to stick the samples onto the painting as independently as possible.

PLENARY

Bring everyone back to the semicircle with their artwork. Ask each child to come to the front to show their artwork and compare it to the original piece.

CONSOLIDATION ACTIVITIES

Repeat this process with other famous pieces of artwork or for art related to a class topic.

27. Im-press Me! Part 2

Learning Objective

Developing

Pupils practise new skills with less support, developing their knowledge of the process of making.

Additional Skills

Kinaesthetic: moving around in new environments.

Fine motor: using a pincer grip to select foliage.

Attention: recalling a process and activity from a previous day or week.

Resources

Large copies of Monet's painting *Water Lilies*

Colour bingo board to match the colours found in the painting

A4 printer paper

Heavy books

PVA glue

Glue spreaders

MAIN

- Repeat the steps in 'Im-press Me! Part 1' up to the last bullet point.

- Once back in the classroom support the children to come and sit back in the semicircle.

- Sit in front of the group and show them the flowers/leaves/plants they have collected to match the colours in the painting. Explain that we are going to dry the flowers/leaves/plants so the artwork lasts longer.

- Model taking a piece of A4 printer paper and folding in half, placing e.g. the petals of a flower in the middle of the paper and then placing the folded paper in the middle of a heavy book. Show a previously made example of a dried petal.

- Support children to sit at the table and place their collected flowers/plants/leaves in folded A4 printer paper and inside heavy books.

- Support the children to check on their flower presses over the next few days.

- When the flowers/leaves/plants are dry support the children to stick them onto the large copies of the painting, matching the colours to make their own artwork.

PLENARY

Support the children to come to the front of the class and show their artwork to their friends, comparing it to the original piece.

CONSOLIDATION ACTIVITIES

Repeat the flower pressing process for other famous paintings or artwork related to the class topic.

28. Shady Names

Learning Objective

Developing

Pupils start to use tools and simple actions to produce a piece of work.

Additional Skills

Fine motor: using a palmer or tripod grip to manipulate a mark making tool.

Attention: maintaining attention in a small group for up to 10 minutes.

Social communication: taking turns as part of a small group.

Resources

Blu Tack

Interactive whiteboard (IWB)

Letter template cards for the first letter of the name of each child in the group

Child-safe mirrors

Whiteboards and whiteboard pens for each child

Pencils

MAIN

• To set up this activity Blu Tack the letter template cards onto the wall or the IWB at the front of the class.

• Support the small group to come and sit in a semicircle in front of the letter cards ready to learn.

• Choose a child in the group. Support them to look in the mirror and sing the hello song to the tune of 'Farmer's in the Den': 'Look in the mirror, look in the mirror, look in the mirror, Child's name is here today!'

• Then support the child to mark make on their whiteboard and then to come to the front of the group and show their mark making.

• Then give the child a pencil and support them to identify the first letter of their name and to use a shading or line drawing technique to fill in their letter, e.g. cross-hatching, zigzag lines.

• Repeat this for all the children in the group.

• When the children are familiar with this activity it could be done as a race, e.g. first child to mark make on their whiteboard, bring it to the front, find their name letter and fill it in is the winner!

PLENARY

When all the children have made their marks, choose a child to come to the front. Support the child to count how many children are here today and to make tally marks using the pens to represent the number of children present.

CONSOLIDATION ACTIVITIES

Make different art pieces out of the letters of the children's names, e.g. they could paint over the letters, use pastels to colour the letters in, etc. and then make a display out of the letters in the classroom.

29. Face of Clay

Learning Objective

Securing

Working in 2D or 3D, pupils may intentionally represent an emotion. Pupils make appropriate use of tools and materials.

Additional Skills

Fine motor: handling tools and materials purposefully to make a meaningful shape.

Tactile: touching and experiencing different sensory media such as clay.

Attention: maintaining attention to complete an activity for 20 minutes or more.

MAIN

- Support the children to look at their face in the mirror and identify facial features and the shapes that they see.

- Support the children to sing the song 'If you're happy and you know it' and make different emotional faces in the mirrors as part of the song, e.g. 'If you're sad and you know it turn your mouth down.' 'If you're angry and you know it scrunch up your face.'

- Explain that today we are going to make faces that represent how we feel out of clay using different tools.

- Model choosing an emotion from the symbols and then using the rolling pin to flatten two pieces of clay.

- Then model choosing a shape cutter from the shape symbols, e.g. the circle, and using it to cut two circles from one of the pieces of clay to make 'eyes', then model rolling a piece of clay into a sausage shape, placing it upside down for the mouth and labelling their creation 'sad face'.

- Support the children to do the same until they have made one or two self-portraits from clay, representing different emotions.

- Take a picture of the finished face and the face of the child imitating the emotion they have chosen.

PLENARY

Lay out the children's clay faces on a table top and give each child a copy of the pictures of themselves and their friends making the faces of the emotions they chose to create. Support the children to match the photos to the clay self-portraits.

29. Face of Clay *cont.*

Resources

Mirrors

Visuals of different types of emotions, e.g. 'happy', 'sad', 'angry', etc.

Rolling pins

Modelling clay

Shape cutters in the shapes of circle, triangle and semicircle

Camera

Visuals of shapes of shape cutter, e.g. triangle, circle symbols

CONSOLIDATION ACTIVITIES

Set up the clay with the shape cutters and emotion symbols during a choosing session or outside and encourage the child to use the shape cutter tools as independently as possible to explore making different clay faces representing different emotions.

30. Four Trees

Learning Objective

Securing

Pupils develop their ideas and work in 2D.

Additional Skills

Auditory: listening to instructions.

Attention: working for 20–25 minutes.

Fine motor: working with a range of tools.

Resources

Four squares of paper for each child

Pencils

Felt tips

Pastels

Paint

MAIN

- Provide each child with a square of paper and a pencil. Ask them to draw a tree. (Have pictures of trees on the table if needed.)

- Collect all the pictures in (ensure that each one is named).

- Again, give each child a square of paper and ask them to draw another tree. This time provide them with felt tips to create their work.

- Collect these in.

- On a third sheet of paper, ask children to draw another tree and use pastels to create their work.

- Collect these in.

- Finally, on a fourth sheet of paper, ask children to draw a tree and use paint to create their work.

PLENARY

Leave all of the work on the drying rack to dry and ask the children to tidy up the resources.

CONSOLIDATION ACTIVITIES

Once the work is dry, hand out each of the four pieces of work to the children and ask them to order them ready for mounting.

31. Piece It Together

Learning Objective

Securing

Pupils know that paintings have meaning.

Additional Skills

Communication: asking and answering questions.

Attention: working for 20–25 minutes.

Visual: noticing detail.

Resources

Access to computer and interactive whiteboard

Image of famous painting

Same image cut into pieces and laminated to make a 'jigsaw'

MAIN

- Prior to the lesson, spend time selecting a painting that you feel the children could talk about, but that you also enjoy looking at. Avoid anything too abstract at this point as the children will benefit from concrete reference points within the painting.

- Have the painting displayed on the interactive whiteboard as the children come and join the group.

- Ask the children to look closely at the painting for a few moments. Then ask them some questions about what they think it is about.

- Hand out the pieces of the painting jigsaw to each of the children.

- Spend time asking the children about the piece they have, what they can see and if they can match it to the larger painting.

- One by one the children are encouraged to stand up and talk about their piece and show the rest of the group where it would fit. Each child places their piece of jigsaw onto a large piece of paper, ready to replicate the painting.

- Repeat for everyone in the group.

PLENARY

Take a look at the painting on the whiteboard and the painting jigsaw; are all the pieces in the correct place? If they need moving, ask a child if they can come and 'fix' the painting.

CONSOLIDATION ACTIVITIES

Place some art books in the book corner so that the children can explore paintings, sculptures and drawings by different artists from different time periods.

32. Outdoor Observations

Learning Objective

Securing

Pupils communicate ideas and experiences through their use of colour, form, line and tone.

Additional Skills

Visual: looking at an object in the environment and re-creating it on paper.

Tactile: using different art media to create colour and lines.

Attention: maintaining attention for 20–25 minutes to complete a piece of work.

Resources

Slideshow or images of objects found in the outside environment, e.g. trees, playground equipment, etc.

Sketchbooks

Symbols to represent the different art media

Different art media such as paint, pastels, charcoal and pencils

Large pieces of white paper

MAIN

• Support the children to sit in a semicircle ready to learn.

• Show the group the images of objects found in the outside environment and explain we are going outside to sketch our favourite objects.

• Model choosing an art media from the art media symbols, e.g. the charcoal, choosing an image of an outside object, e.g. the swing, and opening the sketchbook and using the charcoal to make an image of the swing using lines.

• Then support the children to choose an art media; collect their sketchbooks and head outside to choose an object to draw.

• Support the children to think about the lines and colours of the objects to make as accurate a re-creation as possible.

PLENARY

Count down '5, 4, 3, 2, 1, outside has finished; time to come back to the classroom.' Back in the semicircle support the children to come to the front of the class and show their sketches to the group and use language/symbols/sign to describe their observations.

CONSOLIDATION ACTIVITIES

In the next lesson support the children to look through their sketchbooks, choose their favourite sketch and re-create this on the large white paper, possibly using different art media.

33. Tall Towers

Learning Objective

Securing

Pupils develop their ideas and use materials and processes working in 2D and 3D.

Additional Skills

Tactile: manipulating clay to form a structure.

Communication: communicating ideas to another person.

Visual: creating a structure using a design as a guide.

Resources

Images of tall, iconic towers that have small bases, e.g. the Shard, the Gherkin, etc.

Paper

Pencils

Small square pieces of card

Clay

Tools for manipulating clay

MAIN

- Support the children to sit in a semicircle ready to learn.

- Show the group the images of the iconic tall towers and explain that they have small bases but are still tall. See if the children recognise any of the buildings.

- Explain that the children are going to design their own tall tower by drawing it first and then they are going to make it out of clay to see if it will stand up.

- Support the children to move to the tables and to use the pencils and paper to design their own tall towers.

- Once the children have designed the towers, give each child the small square piece of card and some clay.

- Support the children to build the tower they have designed using the small square piece of card as a base.

PLENARY

Support the children to bring their completed towers back to the semicircle at the end of the lesson. Ask each child in turn to come to the front, show their drawn design and then their 3D tower, and support the child to talk about their building.

CONSOLIDATION ACTIVITIES

Repeat this activity for other iconic architectural buildings, possibly linked to other topics, e.g. castles, Victorian buildings, etc.

34. On Your Bike!

Learning Objective

Securing

Pupils purposefully choose colours.

Additional Skills

Gross motor: pedalling and directing a bike.

Kinaesthetic: using controlled movement to create a piece of art.

Communication: communicating a choice to another person.

Resources

Access to a large space

Large pieces/rolls of paper

Masking tape

Large trays/builder's trays

Scooters

Pedal bikes

Different coloured paints

Images of Jackson Pollock paintings

Symbols to match the paint colours

Glue sticks

Video camera

MAIN

- To set up this activity, place the large pieces/roll of paper on the floor of the large space and tape it down using the masking tape. Place the builder's trays next to the paper and line up the scooters and bikes. Place the paint bottles on a table next to the builder's trays.

- At the start of the lesson, show the children the images of the Jackson Pollock paintings (if possible go to a gallery to see the paintings in real life). Ask the children to identify the colours that they can see using speech/sign/symbols.

- Explain we are going to make paintings that look like the images but using bikes and scooters to do the painting! Model choosing a paint colour, squeezing some into a builder's tray, choosing a bike or scooter, covering the wheels in the paint and then whizzing up and down the large paper to create lines and patterns as seen in the images.

- Support the children to choose colours and scooters or bikes to take part in creating their own Jackson Pollock images.

- If possible film the children taking part in this activity so they can watch the video at a later date.

PLENARY

After allowing the children to choose different colours to create their images on the large paper, count down '5 ,4, 3, 2, 1, painting has finished!' Then give the children colour symbols and ask them to label the colours on the painting by sticking the colour symbol next to an example of that colour using the glue sticks. Use the large images as display backing paper!

CONSOLIDATION ACTIVITIES

Whenever possible support the child to make choices for colours in other subjects, e.g. during topic work support the child to choose the colours needed to make their map in Geography.

35. Mosaic Mural

Learning Objective

Securing

Pupils finish a piece of work following an established pattern of activity.

Additional Skills

Social communication: working as part of a larger group to complete a piece of art.

Attention: recalling skills and resources from a previous lesson/day/week.

Fine motor: using skills such as cutting and pincer grip to manipulate small pieces of art media.

Resources

Images of mosaic murals from around the world

A large wall space in the classroom or school (could be a whole display board in classroom or corridor)

Backing paper

Pencils

Coloured card

Scissors

PVA glue

Glue sticks

Trays or boxes for packing away the resources ready to be used during the next session

Cameras/electronic tablets

MAIN

- Explain to the whole group that we have a very exciting project to make a mosaic mural for our display. Show the children the images of mosaic murals from around the world and explain that the large pictures are made from lots of tiny pieces of coloured tile. Show the children the large wall space and explain that as a group we are going to choose a large picture to fill the space using lots of tiny pieces of coloured card and that we need to choose a large picture all together.

- The large picture could be chosen from a pre-selected range of images relating to the class topic, paintings by a famous artist or the class could design their own pictures and the children vote on their favourite.

- Once the large image has been selected draw out the image on backing paper on the large wall space using a pencil.

- The class then work together over several sessions to select the appropriate coloured card to cut up and stick to the mural using the PVA glue or glue sticks.

PLENARY

The completed image will take several sessions to complete, so at the end of each session the children need to pack away the resources and then find them and use them again at the beginning of the next session until the big picture has been created.

CONSOLIDATION ACTIVITIES

Once the large mural has been completed encourage the children to use cameras/electronic tablets to take photos of their hard work and then to present them to the rest of the school or Key Stage during an assembly; working together to create such a big piece of art is a massive achievement!

36. Cointastic

Learning Objective

Securing

Pupils can work in 2D to intentionally represent or symbolise an object or emotion.

Additional Skills

Social communication: recognising and representing different emotions.

Fine motor: using a tripod grip to manipulate art media.

Attention: moving attention from one activity to another within the same session.

Resources

A range of coins

A4 white paper

Symbols for silver, bronze/brown, gold

Wax crayons that match the colour of the coins (metallic wax crayons)

Scissors

Emotion symbols for happy, sad, ok

Glue sticks

Large pieces of card

MAIN

- Support the children to come and sit facing the lead adult ready to learn.

- Explain that today we are going to be describing how we feel with our art!

- First demonstrate choosing a coin, e.g. a 2p piece, selecting the correct colour wax crayon (first from the colour symbols and then matching to the correct colour wax), placing the paper over the top and using the wax crayon to rub over the coin to make a wax rubbing of the coin. Repeat this for several more coins.

- Then model using the scissors to cut out the coins and model choosing an emotion from the emotion symbols, e.g. 'happy'.

- Model using the glue stick to make a happy face out of the cut-out coin rubbings by sticking them on the large piece of card.

- Support the children to move to the tables to follow the steps made by the lead adult to create their own coin faces.

PLENARY

Once the children have completed their artwork support the group to come back to the semicircle. Ask each child to come to the front to show their work and the other children identify the emotion they have expressed using the coin rubbings.

CONSOLIDATION ACTIVITIES

Repeat this activity by making rubbings of different items, e.g. leaves, sensory balls, etc., and extend the range of emotions the children can choose from to represent.

37. Gallery Gander

Learning Objective

Securing

Pupils communicate ideas and experiences through their use of colour, form, line and tone.

Additional Skills

Kinaesthetic: moving around confidently in a new/unfamiliar environment.

Visual: showing a preference for a piece of art or sculpture.

Social communication: explaining ideas to another person.

Resources

Access to a local art gallery

Risk assessments and any other items needed for a visit outside school

Slideshow explaining what to expect on the trip

Sketchbooks

Pencils

Crayons

Cameras/electronic tablets

MAIN

- Plan a trip to a local art gallery. Prepare the children for the trip using a slideshow to show them where they are going and what to expect to happen whilst they are there.

- Explain to the children that they are going to take their sketchbooks and while they are at the gallery they are going to choose their favourite paintings and/or sculptures and use pencils and crayons to re-create their chosen paintings/sculptures in their sketchbooks. Explain that the children will also take a photo of their chosen paintings/sculptures.

- Support the children to go to the local art gallery and explore the paintings and sculptures. Encourage the children to choose preferred paintings/sculptures and try to explain reasons for their choice, e.g. 'I like the colours.' 'I like the people in the painting.'

- Support the children to look closely at their chosen pieces of art and to re-create them in their sketchbooks, paying particular attention to the colours and lines of the artwork. Support the children to use the cameras/tablets to take photos of their chosen pieces of art.

PLENARY

Once the trip is over and everyone is back in the classroom, ask each child in turn to come to the front of the class and show the photos of their chosen artwork and then their sketches. Support the children to describe their drawings and why they chose those particular paintings or sculptures to draw.

37. Gallery Gander *cont.*

CONSOLIDATION ACTIVITIES

During other subjects encourage the children to pay particular attention to colours, lines and shapes in anything that they are creating on paper, e.g. the lines used to create letters and numbers, the colours in a book, the shapes that make up a larger image such as a face.

Teaching note: if a local art gallery is not accessible explore a famous art gallery online: take a virtual tour of the Uffizi Gallery, for example.

38. Shady Shadows

Learning Objective

Securing

Pupils use a growing art vocabulary.

Additional Skills

Fine motor: using a tripod grip to make different effects.

Attention: maintaining attention on an activity for 20–25 minutes.

Communication: communicating ideas to another person.

Resources

Large wall space

Large white paper

Blu Tack/masking tape

Overhead projector (OHP)

Range of objects that will create an interesting shadow, e.g. bowls, plates, 2D shapes, etc.

Pencils

Charcoal

Previously made shadow images using shading techniques such as hatching and cross-hatching

MAIN

- To set up this activity tape the large white paper to the large wall space and set up the OHP opposite so that it casts light onto the paper. Place the range of objects and the pencils and charcoal on a table next to the OHP.

- Support each child to come over to the OHP and model choosing and placing an object onto the OHP so that it casts a shadow onto the large white paper.

- Model taking, e.g. a pencil, and then using vocabulary and technique such as 'shading', 'cross-hatching' and 'hatching' to shade in the shadow of the object onto the white paper. Turn off the OHP to show the child that they have created the image of the object on the paper.

- Then support the child to choose an object, place it on the OHP and use pencils or charcoal and shading techniques and vocabulary, such as 'hatching' or 'cross-hatching', to create the shadow images on the paper.

PLENARY

Once the child has created several different shadow images using shading techniques support them to come to the table to look at the previously made shadow images. Talk about the images together and support the child to identify different techniques such as hatching and cross-hatching.

CONSOLIDATION ACTIVITIES

Repeat this activity to use and consolidate language when talking about lines, e.g. diagonal, horizontal, vertical, zigzag and when learning about form and shape, e.g. circle, square, etc.

39. Still Life

Learning Objective

Securing

Pupils know that paintings and drawings have meaning.

Additional Skills

Social communication: recognising and expressing an emotion.

Communication: communicating ideas and experiences to others.

Attention: maintaining attention for 25 minutes or more and over several sessions.

Resources

Still life pictures by famous artists of objects, e.g. examples of Paul Cezanne's work, Pablo Picasso's work, etc.

Still life objects that are meaningful to the child (could be sent in from home), e.g. teddy bear, favourite book, favourite food, etc.

Art materials, e.g. watercolours, pastels, pencils, crayons, etc.

Paper

Blu Tack

Easels (if available)

MAIN

- Support the children to sit with a view of the examples of the famous artists' work on easels or on the wall.

- Explain the work of the artists, showing the media used (paint, pastel, etc.) and explaining that the objects are arranged in a certain way to create the piece of art.

- Explain that the children are going to create their own pieces of 'still life' art using the objects that are meaningful to them.

- Support the children to explore and identify their objects and to experiment with different ways of arranging them whilst referring to the work of the famous artists.

- Once the children have decided on the best way to arrange their objects, support them to choose the art media they wish to work in and to then create their piece of still life art by drawing their arrangements.

PLENARY

Place the pieces of still life art back on the easels or on the walls and invite another class/members of the leadership team/parents to come to the class gallery. Support the children to explain their art to the other people, explaining why the objects are meaningful to them, why they have arranged them in the way that they did and why they chose to work in, e.g., paint, pastels, etc.

CONSOLIDATION ACTIVITIES

Support the children to look at other pieces of artwork that have meaning, e.g. Leonardo Da Vinci's *Mona Lisa* and repeat this lesson, re-creating the meaning behind the paintings with relevance to their own lives, e.g. placing a photo of a loved one looking happy on a fantasy background and then creating this as a piece of art in watercolours.

DESIGN AND TECHNOLOGY

40. Build It Up

Learning Objective

Emerging

Pupils, with help, begin to assemble components provided for an activity.

Additional Skills

Social communication: sharing an experience.

Attention: building attention towards 5–7 minutes.

Visual: copying adult.

Resources

LEGO® bricks

LEGO® instructions for a simple build, or create some by taking photos

MAIN

- Either using the instructions from the LEGO® set, or the ones you have created, provide these and five to seven pieces of LEGO® for each child and the same for the adult.

- Sit the child facing the adult with a table in between them.

- Point to the first instruction and select the corresponding LEGO® brick. Verbally encourage the child, or hand under hand (adult's hand on bottom, child's on top) select the same piece for the child.

- Repeat until the model has been built. Encourage the child to take a turn independently as you move through the activity.

PLENARY

Write the child's name on a piece of card and place this and their model on a display table.

CONSOLIDATION ACTIVITIES

Leave simple instructions in the LEGO® box so that the children can look at them as they are exploring the bricks.

41. Tumble Down

Learning Objective

Emerging

Pupils, with help, begin to assemble components provided for an activity.

Additional Skills

Gross motor: making larger movements to lift and move big blocks.

Social communication: watching the actions of another person.

Kinaesthetic: moving around confidently in a different environment.

Resources

Access to a soft play room or large space with mats

Visual of the soft play room/large space (object or symbol)

Large soft play blocks

Visual (object or symbol) for the next activity, e.g. classroom, playground, etc.

MAIN

• Support each child to accompany you to the soft play room or the large space with mats, showing them the visual so that they understand where they are going.

• Model using the large soft play blocks to build a structure, e.g. a tower, a house, etc., and then running into it to knock it down!

• Support the child to use the large soft play block to build their own structure and then run into it to knock it down!

PLENARY

When it is time to finish the lesson, count down '5, 4, 3, 2, 1, soft play has finished; time to tidy up.' Adult and child place the large soft play blocks in a tidy pile in the corner of the room ready for the next session. Support the child to hold the visual for the next activity while they walk to the next session.

CONSOLIDATION ACTIVITIES

Place large soft play blocks or wooden blocks in the outside play area and encourage the child to explore building and knocking down different structures as independently as possible.

42. Pack a Picnic

Learning Objective

Emerging

Pupils explore options within a limited range of materials.

Additional Skills

Attention: building attention towards 5–7 minutes.

Fine motor: using tools to spread/grate.

Communication: requesting favourite fillings.

Resources

Bread

Sandwich fillings (e.g. jam, cheese, cucumber, hummus)

Butter

Plates

Table knives

Grater

MAIN

- Prior to this session, check on any allergy or food preferences for the children in the group, and plan ingredients accordingly.

- First ask everyone to go and wash and dry their hands ready to do cooking.

- Present the group with the range of options for the sandwich fillings.

- Model taking two slices of bread, spreading butter with a knife and choosing a filling, finally cutting the sandwich into four.

- Ask each child what they would like in their sandwich.

- Provide the child with the ingredients and equipment that they will need to make their sandwich.

- Support the children with the tasks such as spreading or grating where needed.

PLENARY

Once all the sandwiches have been made, the adults tidy the leftover ingredients whilst the children eat.

CONSOLIDATION ACTIVITIES

On a sunny day, or a planned trip, carry out this activity again in the morning; reduce adult support over time. Being able to make a snack is a key life skill so carrying out this activity multiple times will be very beneficial.

43. Winter Flakes

Learning Objective

Emerging

Pupils contribute to activities, coactively grasping and moving simple tools.

Additional Skills

Attention: building attention towards 5–7 minutes.

Fine motor: using a hole punch.

Resources

White paper

Hole punch

Scissors

MAIN

- Provide each child with a pre-folded piece of paper (folded two to four times depending on ability).

- Give each child a hole punch. One child at a time, hand under hand (i.e. adult's hand on the hole punch, child's hand on top of adult's), punch holes in the paper.

- Adult removes their hand and verbally prompts child to take a turn themselves.

- Support the next child in the same way.

- Once everyone has punched holes in their paper, take one of the pieces of paper and cut the edges to create a snowflake pattern.

- Gain the child's attention by saying their name and open the folded paper in front of them saying, 'Wow, you made a snowflake!'

- Repeat for everyone in the group.

PLENARY

This is a good opportunity to develop a pincer grip by asking the children to help pick up any holes that have fallen on the floor. Count down and finish the activity.

CONSOLIDATION ACTIVITIES

Place a large piece of paper out with white, silver and light blue paint and brushes. Encourage the children to come and add marks to the paper. Use this as the backing paper for a winter display. The snowflakes can then be added to this along with any other winter work you do.

44. Cut, Roll, Shape

Learning Objective

Emerging

Pupils use a basic tool with support.

Additional Skills

Attention: building attention towards 7–10 minutes.

Fine motor: using a range of tools.

Communication: negotiating sharing equipment.

Resources

Aprons

Simple no-cook play dough recipe (or play dough from 'Roll the Dough' activity)

Rolling pins

Table knives

Pastry cutters

MAIN

- Everyone should wear an apron.
- Provide each child with a piece of play dough (or quickly make some as a group).
- Place the tools in the centre of the group.
- Each child should take a tool and begin exploring.
- Name the action that the child is carrying out ('cutting', 'rolling', etc.).
- Encourage the children to try a range of tools and to share their favoured ones.

PLENARY

After around 5 minutes count down from 5 to 0 and support the children to tidy up.

CONSOLIDATION ACTIVITIES

When doing this activity another time, add scissors so that the children can practise scissor skills cutting strips of play dough.

45. Guess Who?

Learning Objective

Emerging

Pupils demonstrate preferences for materials.

Additional Skills

Attention: building attention towards 7–10 minutes.

Fine motor: using a pincer grip to pick up small items.

Tactile: exploring a range of textures.

Resources

Range of eyes (cut out, googly, etc.) in labelled bowl

Range of mouths in labelled bowl

Range of noses, ears, hair, etc. with labels as above

Aprons

Large oval for each child

Sellotape

Glue sticks

PVA glue and spreader

Pen

MAIN

• Prior to the children coming into the room, place all of the facial components into labelled bowls (i.e. all eyes in one bowl with label, all mouths in another labelled bowl).

• Everyone should wear an apron.

• Provide each child with an oval that is going to be the face. Leave sellotape, glue stick and PVA glue and a spreader next to each child.

• Allow the children to select the components they want for their face and their preferred sticking method.

PLENARY

After around 7 minutes, everyone stops the activity. Pack all the pieces away and ask children to name their face and put on the art tray to dry.

CONSOLIDATION ACTIVITIES

Once all the faces are dry, have a circle time where the children share their faces with the group and tell everyone what the name of their face is, and how they made it.

46. Roll the Dough

Learning Objective

Emerging

Pupils use a basic tool with support.

Additional Skills

Attention: building attention towards 7–10 minutes.

Fine motor: using two hands to mix and stabilise.

Communication: requesting favoured colour.

Resources

Aprons

Simple no-cook play dough recipe

Ingredients for the play dough

Bowls

Spoons

Range of food colouring

MAIN

- Everyone should wear an apron.
- Present to the group the simple instructions to make a no-cook play dough.
- Ask the children each to take a bowl and spoon.
- All together, follow the instructions to make the play dough. Encourage the children to use two hands, one to stabilise the bowl and one to use the spoon to mix.
- Once everyone has made a dough of the correct consistency, ask each child what colour they would like.
- Support adding the food colouring and doing the final mix.
- Allow the children time to explore their play dough, rolling and squashing.

PLENARY

After around 5 minutes of exploring the dough, count down from 5 to 0 and support the children to tidy up and wash their hands.

CONSOLIDATION ACTIVITIES

Add play dough to an exploration tray, such as the beach. The children can add shells, seaweed, etc. to the play dough and leave it to dry.

47. Eat Me!

Learning Objective

Emerging

Pupils use a basic tool with support.

Additional Skills

Fine motor: grasping and handling tools for eating.

Tactile: experiencing different tastes and smells.

Social communication: taking part in a small group activity.

Resources

A range of fruits

Symbols to match the fruits

Child-safe cutlery such as knives, forks and spoons

Chopping boards

Bowls

MAIN

- Check for any allergies prior to this session.
- Everyone should wash and dry hands before sitting at the table.
- Support the children to sit at the table facing the lead adult.
- Model choosing a fruit, e.g. a banana, and labelling it using speech and showing the symbol.
- Then model peeling the banana and using the knife to chop it up and placing the pieces in a bowl. Repeat for another fruit, e.g. an apple.
- Support the children to select fruits and use the cutlery to chop it up and then eat their fruit salads.
- Encourage the children to indicate if they like or don't like the fruits they have chosen.

PLENARY

Once the children have finished making and eating their fruit salads, count down '5, 4, 3, 2, 1, finished; it's time to tidy up.' Support the children to use the cutlery to scrape any remaining fruit into the bin and then to use a sponge to wash up their bowl and cutlery.

CONSOLIDATION ACTIVITIES

At other times across the day, support the child to use basic tools such as cutlery to access eating food, e.g. at lunchtime use a knife and fork to cut food and a spoon to eat pudding.

48. Bang Bang!

Learning Objective

Developing

Pupils watch others using a basic tool and copy the action.

Additional Skills

Attention: building attention towards 10–15 minutes.

Fine motor: holding a hammer and nail.

Communication: following instructions.

Visual: accurate hand and eye coordination.

Resources

Block of wood

Nails

Hammer

MAIN

- This activity should be done on a one to one basis.

- Present a block of soft wood to the child and allow them to touch it (ensure that it is suitable for classroom use, e.g. no splinters).

- Show the child a nail and the hammer.

- Model holding the nail vertical to the wood and resting the hammer on the head of the nail, lifting the hammer slightly and making a small tap on top of the nail. Repeat until the nail is deep enough into the wood not to require holding.

- Hand under hand (adult's hand on bottom, child's on top) support the child to position the nail and get a feel for how much pressure should be applied with the hammer.

- Once the child has taken a few turns like this, watch the child closely to ensure that they do not apply too much pressure. Praise them for accurate, soft taps of the nail.

- Repeat with two to three nails, encouraging the child's increasing independence.

PLENARY

After around 10 minutes, count down from 5 to 0 and end the activity. Ask the child to help safely put the equipment away.

CONSOLIDATION ACTIVITIES

Place toys out that require accurate hammer hits (such as Ball Pound) so that the children can practise away from the real hammer and nail activity.

49. Veg Print

Learning Objective

Developing

Pupils watch others using a basic tool and copy the action.

Additional Skills

Tactile: smelling and feeling different fruits and vegetables.

Social communication: imitating the action of another person.

Resources

Play dough or clay

Tools for working with clay, e.g. child-safe knife, rolling pin

Range of fruits and vegetables

Symbols to match the fruits and vegetables

MAIN

- Support each child to come and sit opposite you at the table.

- Model rolling out the play dough/clay using the rolling pin, selecting a vegetable or fruit and then pressing it into the play dough/clay to leave a print. Verbally label the print, e.g. 'avocado'. Use the knife to cut out the print and put the print to one side.

- Give the child a clump of play dough/clay and repeat this activity, encouraging the child to look at you and imitate your actions throughout.

PLENARY

Line up all the play dough/clay prints on the table and support the child to use the symbols to match the correct fruit or vegetable to the print.

CONSOLIDATION ACTIVITIES

Use the basic tools such as the knife and rolling pin in other activities across the day, e.g. during lunchtime to cut up food, during cooking activities, to explore wet sand, etc.

50. Smooooooothie

Learning Objective

Developing

Pupils demonstrate preferences for ingredients.

Additional Skills

Tactile: smelling and tasting different fruits and vegetables.

Fine motor: using a basic tool such as a knife to cut up fruits and vegetables.

Visual: understanding the cause and effect of operating a machine.

Resources

Range of fruits and vegetables

Paper symbols to match the fruits and vegetables (several copies)

Blank ingredient list (A4 paper with the numbers 1, 2 and 3 written horizontally)

Glue sticks

Child-safe knives

Chopping boards

Bowls

Cups

Blender

MAIN

- Check for allergies before this session.

- Support the children to wash their hands before coming to sit at the table ready to learn.

- Explain that today we are going to make smoothies! First we need to choose three ingredients to put in our smoothies.

- Support the children to taste the fruits and vegetables and to choose three of them that they would like in their smoothie. Support the children to stick the symbols of their chosen ingredients on their ingredient list.

- Support the children to chop up their chosen fruit and vegetables and place them in the bowl.

- Support the children one by one to come to the front to put their ingredients in the blender along with some water, press the 'on' switch and the 'off' switch when the ingredients are blended and then to pour the smoothie into a cup.

PLENARY

Encourage the children to taste their smoothies and indicate if they like or don't like their creation.

CONSOLIDATION ACTIVITIES

Repeat this activity another day and see if the children still choose the same ingredients. Support them to be as independent as possible when using the basic tools.

Teaching note: if the group size is large it might be better to design one smoothie in small groups to avoid having to wait too long for the blender or, ideally, have more than one blender!

51. Build My Car

Learning Objective

Developing

Pupils recognise familiar products.

Additional Skills

Attention: building attention towards 10–15 minutes.

Fine motor: cutting and painting.

Communication: following instructions.

Resources

Visuals (first cut, second stick, third paint)

3D car template for each child and one for adult

Scissors

Glue stick

Paint

Paintbrushes

Aprons

MAIN

- Place all of the equipment and visuals on the table prior to the children joining the lesson.

- Everyone should wear an apron.

- Model the process. In this example we are making a car, but it can be themed to your topic.

- Show the visual 'first cut' and model cutting out the car template.

- Repeat this for second and third steps of stick and paint.

- Then show children the first visual of 'cut'. If possible without supporting, wait for the children to take the car template and the scissors. If needed, offer verbal prompts and then physical prompts.

- Once everyone has cut out the car, show the second visual 'stick' and, again, wait to see if the children can choose the glue stick to be able to put the car model together. Provide verbal before physical prompt if this is needed.

- Finally, show 'third paint' and again allow the children time to locate the correct products for this task.

PLENARY

After around 10 minutes, or longer if the children are all engaged, stop the activity and ask the children to show their cars to each other. Count down and end the lesson.

CONSOLIDATION ACTIVITIES

Once all the cars are dry, use chalk to draw a road on the playground and encourage the children to role-play driving their cars around the road.

52. I Want That Cake

Learning Objective

Developing

Pupils begin to offer responses to making activities.

Additional Skills

Attention: building attention towards 10–15 minutes.

Fine motor: mixing.

Communication: following instructions.

Visual: making a choice from two pictures.

Resources

Aprons

Recipe and picture for chocolate crispy cakes turned into visuals

Recipe and picture for marshmallow crispy cakes turned into visuals

Ingredients for the recipes

Bowls

Spoons

Cake cases

Baking tray

Access to microwave or cooker

MAIN

• Prior to this lesson, check any allergy or dietary requirements, and adapt the recipes accordingly.

• Show the children the pictures of the two types of crispy cakes, one with chocolate and the other with marshmallow (one will be brown, the other white).

• Ask the children which of the cakes they would like to make.

• Once they have chosen, everyone should wash their hands and put on an apron.

• Show a visual of the equipment that they will need and, without too much prompting, encourage the children to source the resources. (Ensure they are within reach and ideally labelled.)

• Follow the recipe, supporting the children where they need it, and especially where heating is required. (Follow school risk assessments around whether or not the children are allowed to be part of the heating process.)

• Finish the activity by spooning the mixture into cake cases and allowing them to cool.

PLENARY

Children wash up with the support of adults.

CONSOLIDATION ACTIVITIES

Perhaps at the end of the week, enjoy eating the cakes that they have made. Ask if the child likes the choice they made about the flavour.

53. Piece Together

Learning Objective

Developing

Pupils operate familiar products with support.

Additional Skills

Attention: building attention towards 10–15 minutes.

Fine motor: programming Beebot.

Communication: following instructions.

Visual: matching two images.

Resources

Beebots

Large mat with pictures of components of a house (e.g. windows, doors, doorbell, post-box)

Blank house for each child

Large pocket dice with the same pictures as on the mat

MAIN

- Prior to the lesson, ensure that all the Beebots are charged.

- Place a mat on the floor with pictures of the different parts to make a 2D house.

- Sit all the children around the mat and remind/show them how to use the Beebots.

- Roll the dice. The children need to programme their Beebot to the correct component that the dice shows (e.g. window).

- Once the Beebot has reached the corresponding image, give each child the piece of the house. Children put this to one side.

- Repeat until everyone has all the pieces.

PLENARY

Children take their pieces of house to a table, or space on the carpet, and put together their 2D house.

CONSOLIDATION ACTIVITIES

Beebots can be used in this way to teach children the names of tools. Place pictures of tools on the mat; as the children move their Beebots to the picture, name the item and model using it. Then let the children take a turn.

54. Make It Move

Learning Objective

Developing

Pupils use basic tools or equipment in simple processes.

Additional Skills

Attention: building attention towards 15–20 minutes.

Fine motor: using a hammer.

Communication: following instructions.

Visual: hand eye coordination.

Resources

Large paper and pens

Classroom-safe wood

Nails

Hammer

Circles of card or pre-made wheels

MAIN

This lesson follows on from 'Bang Bang!'.

- Ask the children if they can name 'things that move'. Draw these on a large piece of paper and label them.

- If cars, trains, bikes, scooters, trains, etc. are not included, add these to the paper.

- Circle four things (bikes, scooters, etc.) and ask the children what they have in common, or what is the same.

- Many features could be mentioned. Once the children have said 'wheels', circle the wheels on the pictures.

- Provide each child with a piece of wood, nails, hammer and either circles of card or pre-made wheels.

- Support the children to add wheels to the wood and use the hammer and nails safely.

PLENARY

Children can attempt to push around their vehicles. Have they all put the wheels in a place where they move?

CONSOLIDATION ACTIVITIES

Leave out junk modelling with card circles and split pins and encourage the children to make vehicles that move.

55. It's All in the Design

Learning Objective

Developing

Pupils begin to communicate preferences in their designing and making.

Additional Skills

Attention: building attention towards 15–20 minutes.

Fine motor: holding a pen.

Communication: making choices.

Resources

A3 design sheet (boxes for colour, how many wheels, how many doors, pattern, etc.)

Pens

MAIN

- Following on from the 'Make It Move' lesson, provide each child with an A3 design page.

- Model completing a sheet, working through each of the boxes and talking it through with the children.

- Children work through each of the boxes, designing their car part by part with adults supporting where necessary.

PLENARY

Everyone should come together and share their designs, telling each other their favourite parts.

CONSOLIDATION ACTIVITIES

Leave the design sheets out on the writing table and encourage the children to make a second or third design so that they get the chance to explore and learn how to use the design sheets.

56. Creative Carving

Learning Objective

Developing

Pupils begin to offer responses to making activities.

Additional Skills

Communication: indicating a preference for an image.

Fine motor: manipulating a basic tool to create an image.

Tactile: feeling and smelling different vegetables.

Resources

Images of carved pumpkins

Cut-out facial feature shapes

Pumpkin template (one per group/child)

Glue sticks

Pumpkin

Pumpkin-carving kit or child-safe knives

MAIN

- Support the children to sit at the table ready to learn. Show the children the images of the carved pumpkins and ask them if they like or don't like them. Also ask the children how they think the images were made.

- Explain that today we are going to make our own carved pumpkins! Model choosing the facial feature shapes and sticking them on the pumpkin template to make a face design.

- Model cutting open the pumpkin, scooping out the insides using a basic tool such as a spoon and using the knife to carve out the image you have designed.

- Support the children to work in small groups to make a face design, cut open the pumpkin, scoop out the insides and then carve their design.

PLENARY

Once all the pumpkins have been carved, place a lit candle inside (an LED candle works just as well) and turn off all the lights. Support the children to comment on their work, indicating what they like about their designs.

CONSOLIDATION ACTIVITIES

Carve out other images on different vegetables such as potatoes and use these to make paint prints and artwork.

57. A Packet Please

Learning Objective

Securing

Pupils explore familiar products and communicate views about them when prompted.

Additional Skills

Attention: building attention over 25 minutes.

Fine motor: using a pencil.

Communication: giving a view.

Resources

Selection of familiar packages (fast food, food, toys, stationery, etc.)

Real items that would go in the packages (or images)

MAIN

- Show the children a range of familiar packaging that you have collected.

- Ask questions such as 'What is inside?', 'Have you seen it before?', 'What shop does it come from?'

- Provide children with (ideally) the real items, but if that isn't possible then photos, and ask them to select the packaging that corresponds.

- Ask the children why they have chosen it.

PLENARY

Show the children a favoured classroom toy, and ask them to draw the package/box that the toy would be sold in.

CONSOLIDATION ACTIVITIES

Take a trip to the local supermarket, ensuring that school risk assessments and policies are followed. Take a look at the different packaging. Buy some items to create a shop back in the classroom.

58. Model Me

Learning Objective

Securing

Pupils begin to contribute to decisions about what they will do and how.

Additional Skills

Attention: building attention over 25 minutes.

Fine motor: using a range of tools.

Communication: asking and answering questions.

Visual: noticing features of an item.

Resources

Design sheets from lesson 'It's All in the Design'

Junk modelling resources

Wood

Tools (hammer, screwdriver, scissors, glue, etc.)

MAIN

- Using the design sheets from the 'It's All in the Design' lesson, tell the children they are going to manufacture their car.

- Place out a large range of junk modelling items, wood and tools in baskets and put 20 minutes on a timer.

- Support the children by encouraging them to look back at their design whilst encouraging them to make the car as independently as possible.

PLENARY

Everyone should bring their completed car to the circle and share this with the group. Show the car and the design sheet. Encourage other children to ask questions to the child about their work.

CONSOLIDATION ACTIVITIES

Set up a role-play garage/mechanics and have the cars that the children have made as part of this. Include role-play tools, overalls and car repair writing frames.

59. Brunel's Bridges

Learning Objective

Securing

Pupils begin to communicate preferences in their designing and making.

Additional Skills

Social communication: working in a small group to communicate ideas and complete a project together.

Fine motor: manipulating materials to create a sculpture.

Attention: recalling and using previously learnt skills to make a sculpture.

Resources

Images of Isambard Kingdom Brunel's railway bridges

Pictures of children in the group

Paper and pencils

Cardboard

Cardboard rolls

Cardboard boxes

Craft matchsticks

Cotton buds

Masking tape

PVA glue

Glue spreaders

MAIN

- Support the children to come and sit in a semicircle ready to learn.
- Explain that we are going to look at the work of the famous engineer Isambard Kingdom Brunel and show the group the images of the railway bridges he designed and built.
- Explain that the children are going to work in small groups to design their own railway bridge and track and support the children to choose friends to work with by choosing from the pictures of the children in the larger group.
- Then support the groups to look at the images of the bridges and use the paper and pencils to design their own railway bridge and track to go underneath.
- In the small groups children discuss which materials are best to use to build their bridges and track sculpture.
- Children then select these materials and use them to build their railway bridge and track.

PLENARY

Support the children to walk around the room to look at the work of the other groups. Support the children to make positive comments about the other group's work, e.g. 'I like how tall the bridge is,' 'I like the colours of the railway track.'

CONSOLIDATION ACTIVITIES

When the children have finished building their sculptures encourage them to say what they like and don't like about their work. Repeat the activity and support the children to make changes according to their own evaluation of their work.

Teaching note: this lesson may be best taught over several sessions to allow children to explore their creativity.

60. Litter Issues

Learning Objective

Securing

Pupils explore familiar products and communicate views about them when prompted.

Additional Skills

Social communication: expressing a view or opinion to another person and/or within a small group.

Fine motor: using tools to create a 2D design and 3D prototype.

Kinaesthetic: transitioning calmly around different environments within the school/local community.

MAIN

- Support the children to come and sit where they will be able to see the slideshow of images.

- Explain the school has a really big problem! There is always rubbish left in the playground (show slideshow) and none of the bins in the school can go in the playground (show images of bins; explain they are too big/small/too open/easily knocked over, etc.).

- Explain that we need to solve the problem by designing a bin that would go well in the playground; all together discuss what this bin would need, e.g. to be closed, not easily kicked over, not too big, not too small, etc.

- As a group go and explore the playground and use the camera/tablets to take photos of locations for the bins, evidence of the current problem. Use sketchbooks to start making ideas for a solution to the problem.

- Back in the classroom, support children to work in pairs/small groups to make a 2D design for the ideal playground bin. Support the children to discuss with each other ideas about size, colour, construction, etc.

- Then support the pairs/small groups to use the junk modelling resources, tape/PVA glue/glue sticks and paint to make a prototype of their bin.

PLENARY

Once the prototypes have been completed, support the pairs/small groups to share their ideas with a larger group such as the Key Stage or with the leadership team. Encourage the children to express their opinions about their products and why they think theirs would be the best solution to the problem.

60. Litter Issues *cont.*

Resources

Access to a playground (within school grounds or local park)

Slideshow of images of rubbish left in the playground

Slideshow of images of bins around the school and playground

Symbols to support individual children to express their opinions, e.g. 'like', 'don't like', 'too big', 'too small', etc.

Camera/electronic tablet

Sketchbooks

Paper

Pencils

Crayons

Junk modelling resources

Paint

Tape/PVA glue/glue sticks

CONSOLIDATION ACTIVITIES

If possible place the prototypes in the playground and support the children to monitor how they are used and if their product provided a solution to the problem. Identify other issues around the school for which the class could design products to solve the problem.

Teaching note: this lesson would be best taught over several sessions to allow the children to fully develop their ideas.

61. Pop Up Tales

Learning Objective

Securing

Pupils begin to contribute to decisions about what they will do and how.

Additional Skills

Fine motor: manipulating tools such as scissors.

Visual: designing and creating an appealing storybook.

Social communication: sharing their finished product with another child.

Resources

A range of pop up books

A familiar story for the class (a nursery rhyme or fairy tale would be ideal)

Basic storyboard template (e.g. an A4 piece of paper with three empty boxes), one per child

Instructions to make a simple pop up book (around three pages)

Card

Colouring in materials

Scissors

Glue

MAIN

This lesson would work well as a project for half a term.

• Support the children to come and sit in a semicircle ready to learn. Show the children the pop up books and allow them to explore. Encourage the children to comment on the books, e.g. what they like (colours, story), what they don't like (too long, no animals, etc.).

• Explain that we are going to make our own pop up stories to share with a child in another younger class!

• Model looking at a familiar class story (for example Hansel and Gretel) and choosing three scenes from the story and drawing these on the storyboard.

• Then model using the simple instructions to make the first scene into a pop up card (e.g. make the trees pop up and draw Hansel and Gretel on the card).

• Then support the children to work at the table to choose their own scenes from the story and follow the instructions to make their own pop up books.

• Allow the children to explore different methods of making their images pop up and to discuss with adults how they are going to make their stories.

PLENARY

Once the children have completed their storybooks, support them to go to another class with younger children to share their stories with the children. Take photos of the children sharing their stories and look back at these to discuss the process at another time.

61. Pop Up Tales *cont.*

CONSOLIDATION ACTIVITIES

Repeat this process for making cards for different occasions; introduce more complex methods of making pop up cards/books so children have a wider range of processes to choose from.

Teaching note: some children may need a lot of support for this activity. In this case reduce the number of pages they make for their story to just one, or have everyone in the class make just one pop up page and make one long story all together.

62. Perfect Pizza Part 1

Learning Objective

Securing

Pupils begin to communicate preferences in their designing and making.

Additional Skills

Tactile: tasting and experiencing different foods.

Attention: maintaining attention on an activity for up to 35 minutes.

Communication: communicating preferences for different foods.

Resources

Images of pizzas

Range of pizza toppings, e.g. pineapple, tuna, cheese, mushrooms, onions, etc.

Paper symbols to match the pizza toppings (several copies of each)

A4 paper divided into two columns; 'I like...' and 'I don't like...' (one per child)

Glue sticks

Pizza templates (one per child)

Pencils and crayons

MAIN

- Check for any potential allergies prior to this lesson.

- Support the children to come and sit at the table ready to learn.

- Explain that we are going to design our own pizzas! Show the images of the pizzas and encourage the children to discuss what they like and don't like about pizzas.

- Working in smaller groups, support the children to taste the different pizza toppings and to make a note of those ones they like and don't like by writing the word/drawing the topping or sticking a paper symbol in the relevant column.

- Once the children have made their 'like' and 'don't like' lists, support them to design their ideal pizza by drawing it on the pizza templates and sticking on the ingredient list using the paper symbols.

PLENARY

Once all the children have designed their ideal pizza support them to share them with their small groups and encourage everyone to discuss their preferences for the pizza toppings.

CONSOLIDATION ACTIVITIES

Other food products could be designed in this way, e.g. ideal breakfast, best biscuit topping.

63. Perfect Pizza Part 2

Learning Objective

Securing

Pupils use basic tools and equipment in simple processes.

Additional Skills

Attention: recalling information and experiences from a previous session.

Tactile: feeling and tasting different food items.

Fine motor: manipulating tools and equipment to make a final product.

Resources

Aprons

Pizza toppings to match those chosen by the children in 'Perfect Pizza Part 1'

Pizza bases

Tomato sauce and cheese

Symbol instructions for making a pizza, e.g. put sauce on pizza, put cheese on pizza, put toppings on pizza, put pizza in oven, eat pizza

Cooking equipment for making pizzas, e.g. child-safe knives for cutting up toppings, chopping boards, oven, etc.

MAIN

This lesson continues from 'Perfect Pizza Part 1'.

- Support children to wash their hands and put on aprons as independently as possible.

- In the kitchen or cooking space, explain that today we are going to make the perfect pizzas that we designed last lesson! Hand back to the children their perfect pizza designs.

- Support the children to identify and select their toppings and then to follow the symbol instructions to make their pizzas.

- Support the children to use basic cooking tools and equipment safely to add their toppings and to cook their pizzas.

PLENARY

Once the pizzas have been made and cooked, eat them all together and discuss the children's views on their products.

CONSOLIDATION ACTIVITIES

If you have supported the children to design other food products such as the best biscuit, support them to make the biscuit following their design.

64. Our House

Learning Objective

Securing

Pupils, with help, manipulate a wider range of basic tools in making activities.

Additional Skills

Social communication: expressing preferences and views within a small group.

Fine and gross motor: manipulating tools and equipment.

Visual: making decisions for materials based on visual preferences.

Resources

Images of houses and their key features, e.g. windows, doors, curtains, etc.

A very large cardboard box

House template on A3 paper

Material and sewing equipment

Wallpaper samples (if possible, if not could make their own)

Pencils, crayons

Different coloured paints

Painting equipment (rollers, brushes, etc.)

Scissors

Glue

MAIN

This lesson may be best taught over several sessions.

- Support a small group to come and look at the images of houses and identify the key features of the house.

- Explain that we are going to design and make our own house! Show the children the large box and explain that we are going to design the windows, curtains, doors and the inside of the house.

- Support the children to communicate preferences in a small group to design their house using the A3 template. Support the children to explore the material and wallpaper samples so they can make their decisions.

- Support the children to use basic tools to follow their design to make their house, e.g. choose where the doors and windows will go and then use scissors to make them, choose the material for curtains and use scissors and sewing equipment to make them, choose wallpaper samples and use scissors and glue to hang it inside, choose paint colour for the outside of the house and use the paint, rollers and brushes to paint the house.

PLENARY

Once the house has been completed, support the children to discuss if they like or don't like it and how similar it is to the original design. Encourage and support the children to play in the house they have made.

CONSOLIDATION ACTIVITIES

Place the house in the outside area for the children to play in. If other children comment on the house, support the children to explain the processes and tools they used to make it.

65. Habitat

Learning Objective

Securing

Pupils, with help, manipulate a wider range of basic tools in making activities.

Additional Skills

Attention: working as independently as possible to complete a project.

Communication: communicating a preference for materials to another person.

Fine and gross motor: manipulating tools and equipment.

Resources

Images of pets

Images of pet houses, e.g. dog house, hamster house, rabbit run, etc.

Examples of pet houses (dog basket, hamster run, etc.)

Junk modelling resources

Access to the Internet

A4 paper

Pencils

Glue and tape

Scissors

MAIN

This lesson would be best taught over several sessions.

- Support the children to sit so that they have a view of the images of pets.

- Show the images of the pets and ask the children if they have any pets at home (you may need to get this information from parents or carers to support the child's answer).

- Explain that we are going to design a house for our pet (if child doesn't have a pet they can choose their favourite pet animal).

- Look at the examples of the pet houses; how are they put together? What materials are used? Support the children to discuss the things they will need to think about, e.g. size, material, colour, will you need to see inside?

- Support the children to work individually to use the Internet to look up ideas for their pet house and then to use the A4 paper to draw their design.

- Children then use the junk modelling resources as independently as possible to make their pet houses.

- If possible use materials such as lengths of wood, mesh, etc. to make the pet houses and closely support the children to use basic tools such as hammers and small saws to make their pet house.

PLENARY

Support the children to walk around the classroom and look at the completed work of their friends and to make positive evaluations of their work, e.g. 'I like the bright colour of the hamster house.'

CONSOLIDATION ACTIVITIES

If possible, allow the children to take their pet houses home and let their pets explore their prototypes. Encourage the children to share with the class how their pets responded!

66. Landmark Design

Learning Objective

Securing

Pupils begin to contribute to decisions about what they will do and how.

Additional Skills

Communication: informing another person of their intentions.

Fine motor: manipulating small bricks to create a design.

Social communication: able to make positive comments about their own and other people's work.

Resources

Images of famous landmark buildings from a city such as London

Printed images of the landmark buildings (several copies of each)

LEGO® bricks

Paper

Pencils

Camera/electronic tablet

MAIN

- Support the children to have a look at the images of famous landmark buildings. Show the images to the children and support them to identify the buildings.

- Explain that the children are going to choose a building and then make it out of LEGO®. It is up to the children if they want to draw their design first, which bricks they use and how they use them to build a representation of the building.

- Support each child to come and choose an image of a building that they are going to create.

- The children take the image to their table place and carry out the task as independently as possible. Support the children by asking them to explain what they are doing, e.g. putting the big bricks first, making the tower first, etc.

- When children have completed one building, encourage them to come and select another image to make another famous landmark.

- Support the child to take a photo of their completed landmarks.

PLENARY

Once the children have completed their LEGO® landmarks ask them to put them out on the table. Encourage the class to walk around each table and make positive comments about the landmark buildings. Encourage each child to make a comment about their building process.

CONSOLIDATION ACTIVITIES

Print out the photos of the completed buildings and give them to the children. Encourage the children to talk about the activity, how they built their buildings and what they think of them.

MUSIC

67. In the Bag

Learning Objective

Emerging

Pupils use symbols or words to name familiar instruments.

Additional Skills

Social communication: sharing an experience.

Attention: building attention towards 5–7 minutes.

Visual: matching symbol to real object.

Resources

Small drum

Triangle (instrument)

Maraca

Bag

Symbols for each of the instruments

MAIN

• Place the drum, the triangle and the maraca in front of each child. Let them play with each of these instruments.

• Show the symbol of the instrument and say the name as the child explores each one.

• Ask the child to put the instruments in the bag.

• Make a noise with one of the instruments; ask the child either to say the name or find the matching symbol. Adult supports if necessary.

• Repeat.

PLENARY

Play each instrument one last time and put them in the finish box.

CONSOLIDATION ACTIVITIES

Play this game again and this time let the child take a turn holding the bag and making a noise with the instruments so that the adult has to make the guess. Make some incorrect guesses so that the child can correct you!

68. It's Hiding

Learning Objective

Emerging

Pupils begin to look for a noise maker out of sight.

Additional Skills

Social communication: sharing an experience and waiting for a turn.

Attention: building attention towards 5–7 minutes.

Auditory: locating sound in the room.

Resources

'Start' and 'stop' visuals

Box of instruments

MAIN

- Place chairs in a circle and ask everyone to come and join the group.

- Tell the children that they are going to play a game.

- Ask everyone to close their eyes and take an instrument and play it in part of the room, then leave it there and return to the group.

- Ask everyone to open their eyes and see if the children can identify where the sound came from and go and find the instrument.

- Whoever finds it first, takes the next turn.

PLENARY

Once everyone has taken a turn, count down from 5 to 0 and finish the activity.

CONSOLIDATION ACTIVITIES

Play this game regularly so that the children can start identifying the sounds of different instruments.

69. Stop Start Stop

Learning Objective

Emerging

Pupils are aware of cause and effect.

Additional Skills

Social communication: sharing an experience and waiting for a turn.

Attention: building attention towards 5–7 minutes.

Auditory: listening to a request.

Resources

'Start' and 'stop' visuals

Box of instruments

MAIN

- Everyone sits on the carpet. Clap hands and ask the children to join in. Then show the 'stop' visual and model stopping. Then show the 'start' visual and model starting to clap again.

- Place a box of instruments in the centre of the group. Everyone can choose an instrument that they would like to play.

- Give the children a few minutes to explore the sound that their instrument makes and to swap it if they want to.

- Show the 'stop' visual and see if the children are able to follow this request. Repeat a few times with start and stop so that the children become familiar with the concept.

PLENARY

Going around the group, ask each child to make a tune on their instrument and then to place it back in the box.

CONSOLIDATION ACTIVITIES

Leave a selection of instruments as a free choice activity so that the children can explore a wide variety of sounds and actions to make the sounds.

70. App Taps

Learning Objective

Emerging

Pupils are aware of cause and effect.

Additional Skills

Fine motor: using a single finger to tap the screen.

Auditory: listening to the results of their actions.

Visual: understanding where to place finger on screen.

Resources

Electronic tablet

A music app that allows child to touch the keys of a piano/instrument and it plays a sound

MAIN

• Support each child to come and sit with you in a quiet spot.

• Show the child the tablet and demonstrate using the app, acting surprised and happy when a sound is made as a consequence of your action.

• Support the child to explore the app in the same way, calmly making sounds using their finger to press the appropriate place on the screen.

PLENARY

Count down '5, 4, 3, 2, 1, music has finished!' and support the child to put the tablet away and move onto the next activity.

CONSOLIDATION ACTIVITIES

Once the child is familiar with the activity support them to invite another child to come and play with them and practise taking turns to make the instruments play on the tablet.

71. Tap It Out

Learning Objective

Emerging

Pupils attend to familiar musical activities.

Additional Skills

Social communication: sharing an experience.

Attention: building attention towards 5–7 minutes.

Auditory: listening to a beat.

Resources

Small drum

Triangle (instrument)

Maraca

Chimes

Board or cloth

MAIN

- Working in a group of two with an adult, place the drums, triangles, maracas and chimes in the centre of the group and keep a set aside for the adult.

- Allow the children time to play all of the instruments one by one.

- Then place a board or cloth in front of your lap, but so the children can still see your face.

- Choose an instrument (this should be hidden from view) and make a simple rhythm with it.

- Children should listen and then choose the instrument they think the adult is playing and join in.

- Remove the board or cloth, and the children see if they were correct.

- Repeat.

PLENARY

Play each instrument one last time and the children find the matching one and place it in the finish box.

CONSOLIDATION ACTIVITIES

Play this game again and allow each of the children to take a turn at concealing an instrument and making a rhythm that the rest of the group copy.

72. Match It

Learning Objective

Emerging

Pupils listen to a familiar instrument and match the sound.

Additional Skills

Social communication: sharing an experience and waiting for a turn.

Attention: building attention towards 7–10 minutes.

Auditory: matching the correct sounds.

Resources

Box of instruments (one of each instrument for each child, e.g. four triangles, four recorders)

MAIN

• Place chairs in a circle and ask everyone to come and join the group.

• Tell the children that they are going to play a game.

• Place a box of instruments in the centre of the group.

• Ask everyone to close their eyes and take an instrument and give it to one of the members of the group and ask them to play it. Then place this back in the box.

• Ask everyone to open their eyes and to choose the same instrument that was just being played.

• Ask the instrument player if they were correct; if yes, then everyone play together.

• Repeat.

PLENARY

Ask everyone to play a named instrument and put this back in the box; repeat until everything tidied away.

CONSOLIDATION ACTIVITIES

Play this game regularly so that the children can start identifying the sounds of different instruments.

73. Music Man

Learning Objective

Emerging

Pupils pick out a specific musical instrument when asked.

Additional Skills

Social communication: sharing an experience and waiting for a turn.

Attention: building attention towards 7–10 minutes.

Visual: matching the instrument.

Resources

Tune and words for the song 'I Am the Music Man, I Come from Far Away...'

Drums for each child

Triangle and beater for each child

Maracas for each child (or any instruments available)

Stop symbol

Symbols of each of the instruments

MAIN

- Place all the instruments in a basket in the centre of the group with chairs placed around them.

- Adults sit as part of the group. Have the symbols for each of the instruments ready to show the children.

- Adults sing one round of the song; start with 'piano' and everyone models playing an air piano; encourage all the children to join in.

- Show the stop symbol at the end of the round and wait for everyone to finish.

- Show a child in the group two instruments to choose from (or the symbols if able to use these). Once they have chosen, everyone in the group should go to the basket and select the matching instrument.

- All sign a round of the song and play the instrument. Use the stop sign to bring the round to an end.

- Repeat with another child and instrument.

PLENARY

Count down from 5 to 0 and ask everyone to place the instruments back in the basket.

CONSOLIDATION ACTIVITIES

Place out a range of instruments during a free choice activity session; place the accompanying symbols with a stop sign. Adults come and play with the children and encourage the child to use the stop sign with the adult.

74. Reveal Me

Learning Objective

Emerging

Pupils listen to a familiar instrument played behind a screen and match it.

Additional Skills

Social communication: sharing an experience and waiting for a turn.

Attention: building attention towards 7–10 minutes.

Auditory: listening to a sound bite.

Visual: selecting the correct card.

Resources

Interactive whiteboard (IWB)

PowerPoint with slides containing a sound bite of an instrument and a hidden picture of the instrument (six slides in total)

Set of six cards with each instrument for each child

MAIN

• Set the PowerPoint up on the IWB; place chairs around so everyone can see. Invite the children to join you.

• Give each child two of the cards from the sets (the same ones for each child).

• Play the sound bite from the first slide. Repeat this a few times.

• Ask the children to show you what instrument they can hear. Support them to show you the matching card.

• Once everyone has shown their card, reveal the image on the PowerPoint and cheer for everyone who got it right.

• Repeat with another set of two cards and the next instrument on the PowerPoint.

PLENARY

Play a favourite song on the computer and all sing together while the cards are packed away.

CONSOLIDATION ACTIVITIES

Play this game again, increasing the number of cards that the children have to choose from, until they have the whole set of six that they are able to use.

75. Sound It Out

Learning Objective

Emerging

Pupils play loudly, quietly, quickly and slowly.

Additional Skills

Social communication: sharing an experience and waiting for a turn.

Attention: building attention towards 7–10 minutes.

Auditory: following instructions.

Resources

Instrument for each child and adult (minus one)

Visual symbols for 'fast', 'slow', 'loud', 'quiet'

MAIN

• Provide instruments for all members of the group, including the adults, minus one instrument, so that someone is the 'conductor'.

• Lead adult will be the first 'conductor'.

• Choose a visual symbol ('quiet' for example) and present this to the group. Everyone plays their instrument quietly. Model this if children are unsure.

• Everyone swaps instruments around; the person without an instrument becomes the conductor.

• The conductor chooses a symbol to show the group ('loud' for example) and everyone plays their instrument to match.

• Repeat so everyone takes a turn.

PLENARY

Lead adult is the conductor; they clap out a rhythm and everyone copies. Count down and support the children to put the instruments away.

CONSOLIDATION ACTIVITIES

Using a computer program such as Busy Things or an app on an electronic tablet, find a music making game for children to explore making sounds.

76. Sleeping Bunnies

Learning Objective

Emerging

Pupils play loudly and quietly.

Additional Skills

Auditory: responding to an auditory cue.

Social communication: taking part in a small group activity.

Gross motor: controlling large arm movements to create sound.

Resources

Visual symbols for 'loud' and 'quiet'

An Instrument that can be played loudly or quietly for each child, e.g. bells, maracas, etc., in a box

'Sleeping Bunnies' song words

MAIN

- Support the children to come and sit in a semicircle ready to learn.

- Pass the box around the group and verbally label the instrument the child chooses.

- Explain we are going to play our instruments quietly (show symbol and model with instrument) and loudly (show symbol and model with instrument). Everyone practises playing quietly and loudly in response to being shown the symbols.

- Then lead the group in singing the nursery rhyme 'Sleeping Bunnies'.

- Support the children to play their instruments quietly during the first part of the song and in response to the 'quiet' symbol.

- Support the children to play their instruments loudly during the second part of the song and in response to the 'loud' symbol.

PLENARY

Support a child to come to the front to lead the group through the song directing them to play loudly and quietly using the symbols.

CONSOLIDATION ACTIVITIES

Repeat this activity for different nursery rhymes such as 'Twinkle Twinkle Little Star', 'Old MacDonald Had a Farm', etc.

77. Can You Guess?

Learning Objective

Emerging

Pupils listen to a familiar instrument played behind a screen and match it.

Additional Skills

Social communication: sharing an experience and waiting for a turn.

Attention: building attention towards 7–10 minutes.

Auditory: listening to a sound.

Visual: selecting the correct instrument.

Resources

Tray and cloth to cover

Range of instruments and beaters

MAIN

- Place a range of instruments on a tray, show these to the children and then cover the tray with a cloth.

- Ask everyone to close their eyes.

- Make a noise with one of the instruments whilst the children listen.

- Everyone opens their eyes; adult removes the cloth and asks a child to come and show them what instrument they played.

- Allow that child to take a turn.

- Repeat.

PLENARY

Play a favourite song on the computer and everyone uses an instrument to accompany the song, and then tidy away.

CONSOLIDATION ACTIVITIES

Leave this game out as a free choice activity and support two children coming to play.

78. All Join In

Learning Objective

Emerging

Pupils listen to and imitate distinctive sounds played on a particular instrument.

Additional Skills

Social communication: taking part and leading a small group activity.

Fine motor: manipulate a tool to make a sound.

Attention: maintaining attention in a group activity for up to 10 minutes.

Resources

Xylophones and beaters (one instrument and beater per child)

MAIN

- Sit at the front of the group and hand a xylophone and beater to each child.

- Model using a beater to play a key on the xylophone and then say 'All join in!' and encourage the children to copy and play the same key on their instrument.

- Then make more distinctive sounds on the xylophone by running the beater up the keys, say 'All join in!' and encourage the children to make the same distinctive sound.

- Repeat this making different distinctive sounds on the xylophone.

PLENARY

Support a child to come and sit at the front of the group and make a distinctive sound on the xylophone; child uses sign, speech or gesture to indicate that everyone should join in and copy their sound. Repeat this until all the children have had a turn.

CONSOLIDATION ACTIVITIES

Repeat this lesson using different instruments that make very distinctive sounds, e.g. the strings on a guitar, the keys on a piano.

79. Clappity Claps

Learning Objective

Developing

Pupils copy simple rhythms and patterns.

Additional Skills

Social communication: knowing when to take a turn.

Attention: building attention towards 10–12 minutes.

Auditory: noticing changes.

Resources

Visual symbols for 'my turn', 'your turn'

MAIN

• Everyone sits in a circle. Clap a simple 3–4 second pattern. Everyone in the group attempts to copy. Repeat this three times with the same pattern. Use the language 'my turn', 'your turn' to encourage the children to listen before they take a turn.

• Once the children have mastered the idea of the game, go around the circle, with each child taking a turn; encourage the language 'my turn', 'your turn' where possible, or show visual symbols to the group.

• Repeat so that everyone in the group has taken a turn.

PLENARY

Clap out 'goodbye (Name)' to each child and follow the same 'my turn', 'your turn' approach so say and clap, e.g. 'my turn', 'goodbye Kate'. Then say to the children 'your turn', 'goodbye Kate'.

CONSOLIDATION ACTIVITIES

This activity can be repeated with everyone having a drum and beater once they have the idea of listening before they make a sound.

80. How I Play

Learning Objective

Developing

Pupils begin to categorise percussion instruments by how they can be played.

Additional Skills

Fine motor: using a range of beaters to play instruments.

Attention: building attention towards 10–12 minutes.

Visual: finding the matching card.

Resources

Visual symbols for 'shake', 'strike', 'scrape', 'bang'

Set of percussion instruments in a basket

Access to a computer or electronic tablet to play music

MAIN

- Everyone sits in a circle with a basket of instruments in the centre.

- Give each child in the group a visual (e.g. 'scrape', 'shake', 'bang').

- Play a piece of music using a tablet or computer (mix this up so that it includes classical, jazz, rock and roll, etc.). The music does not need to relate to the instruments.

- Stop the music and say 'find your instrument'. Encourage all the children to look in the basket and find an instrument that matches their card.

- Everyone plays their instrument. Go around the group and say, e.g. '(Name) is (shaking)'.

- Place the instruments back in the basket and swap the cards around.

- Repeat.

Teaching note: if playing this game based on how the instruments are used is too hard, include a picture of the instrument on the card, such as 'shake maraca'.

PLENARY

Count down from 5 to 0 and play a piece of relaxing music whilst everyone tidies the instruments away.

CONSOLIDATION ACTIVITIES

You could flip this activity so that everyone has an instrument and they need to find the matching card as to how the instrument can be played (e.g. they have a triangle and so need to find the card that says 'strike').

81. Makes Me Feel

Learning Objective

Developing

Pupils listen to music and can describe it in simple terms.

Additional Skills

Auditory: listening to music.

Attention: building attention towards 15–20 minutes.

Communication: sharing an emotion and potentially a reason.

Resources

Feelings board for each child that contains the symbols for 'happy', 'sad', 'sleepy', 'excited'

Selection of music (heavy rock, classical, jazz, pop, favourite cartoon tune)

Access to a computer or electronic tablet to play the music

MAIN

- Everyone sits in a circle and each child is given a feelings board.

- Play a piece of music and then pause it.

- Ask each child, one at a time, 'How does that make you feel?'

- The children are initially supported to select a feelings card and present this to the lead adult.

- Once there have been a few turns of this and the children have started to get used to the format, ask the whole group 'How does it make you feel?' and see if they can respond at the same time.

PLENARY

Count down from 5 to 0 and play a piece of relaxing music for a few moments of calm before moving on to the next lesson.

CONSOLIDATION ACTIVITIES

More emotions could be added to the feelings board, such as 'frustrated', 'confused', 'worried', etc.

82. Rhythm Response

Learning Objective

Developing

Pupils begin to move expressively in response to music.

Additional Skills

Gross motor: making large, appropriate movements in response to music.

Kinaesthetic: moving around in a large space.

Communication: communicating a feeling through movement.

Resources

Selection of music (heavy rock, classical, jazz, pop, favourite cartoon tune)

Access to a computer or electronic tablet to play the music

Large space

Ribbon wands

Symbols for 'fast' and 'slow'

MAIN

• Support the group to come to the large space.

• Explain that we are going to listen to different types of music and move our bodies and the ribbon wands to the music.

• Model listening to some jazz and move your body and ribbon wand quickly in response to the music. Then play some slower, classical music and show your response by slower movements.

• Give each child and adult a ribbon wand; play the different types of music and encourage the children to respond to the different tempos through their movements.

PLENARY

At the end of the lesson count down '5, 4, 3, 2, 1, dancing has finished.' Support the children to come and lie down on the floor in response to relaxing music to cool down after the lesson.

CONSOLIDATION ACTIVITIES

Take a tablet or CD player outside and encourage the children to respond to different types of music in their movements while they play outside.

83. Reading the Tune

Learning Objective

Developing

Pupils follow simple graphic scores to play a sequence of sounds.

Additional Skills

Auditory: listening to instructions.

Attention: building attention towards 15–20 minutes.

Social communication: responding appropriately in a group situation.

Fine motor: using beaters with percussion instruments.

Resources

Interactive whiteboard (IWB)

Graphic score (see Main)

Instruments (one per child)

MAIN

- Prior to this lesson, create a graphic score. Allocate one instrument per child (each different). Obtain a clip art picture of each of the instruments and create the simple score (e.g. pictures of triangle, triangle, triangle, drum, triangle, tambourine).

- Either place this score on the IWB or print it out on a large piece of paper so that everyone can see this.

- Place chairs around the image and give each child an instrument.

- Start by pointing at the image and the child with the instrument and encouraging them to play. Do this a few times.

- For a fourth turn, point to the image and wait for the child with the corresponding instrument to respond.

PLENARY

Everyone to play their instruments to whatever tune they choose for 2 minutes before the adult counts down and the instruments are put away.

CONSOLIDATION ACTIVITIES

Repeat the activity swapping the instruments around.

84. Run for the Sound

Learning Objective

Developing

Pupils respond to other pupils in music sessions.

Additional Skills

Kinaesthetic: moving quickly with controlled movement in a large space.

Auditory: correctly identifying an instrument and auditory cue.

Social communication: taking part in a large group activity.

Resources

A large space

Five PE mats

Five instruments that can be played loudly

Bingo boards with four squares featuring some of the instruments (one per child)

MAIN

- To set up this activity place the five PE mats around the edges of the room and place one instrument on each mat.

- Support the children to come to the large space ready to start the lesson.

- Explain we are going to play a game where we listen to our friend playing an instrument, look at our bingo card and if that instrument is on the card we run to our friend and give them a high five! Model playing the game (i.e. one stands on a mat, plays the instrument, the other looks at their bingo card, identifies the instrument and then runs to the mat and high fives the adult playing the instrument).

- Choose five children to go and stand on the mats with the instruments and hand out the bingo cards to the remaining children.

- Support the children on the mats to play their instruments one at a time while the other children look at their bingo cards, identify if they have that instrument and, if they do, run to their friend and give them a high five.

- Swap around the children on the mats until everyone has had a turn playing an instrument and running for the sound.

PLENARY

At the end of the lesson support all the children to come and sit on the floor in a circle. Give one child an instrument, such as a drum, and ask them to bang out a rhythm; all the other children clap the rhythm in response to that child.

CONSOLIDATION ACTIVITIES

Repeat this activity in other areas such as the playground. Children could also play this game in pairs so that they can develop their response to others and social communication skills further.

85. Bottle Orchestra Part 1

Learning Objective

Developing

Pupils explore the range of effects that can be made by a sound maker.

Additional Skills

Gross motor: grasping an object.

Auditory: listening out for differences in sounds.

Visual: noticing differences in quantity.

Resources

Aprons

Short video clip of people making music by blowing across the top of bottles

Transparent, empty narrow neck bottles (glass or plastic)

Funnels

Water jugs

Camera/electronic tablet

MAIN

- Support the children to put on aprons and sit with a view of the video clip.

- Explain that today we are going to make music using bottles and show the short video clip.

- Model placing two of the narrow neck bottles on the table, placing the funnel in the neck of one and carefully pouring some water into the bottle. Do the same with the second bottle but add more or less water than the first.

- Model picking up one of the bottles and blowing across the top to make a sound and then doing the same with the second one; do the children notice the difference?

- Support the children to work in pairs or small groups to explore the range of effects different amounts of water have on the sound created by blowing across the top of the bottles.

- Support the children to record their friends making different sounds with the bottles.

PLENARY

At the end of the lesson support the children to carefully pour away all of the water and to come and sit with a view of the IWB. Show the clips of the children making sounds with the bottles and encourage the children to comment on the process and the music they made.

CONSOLIDATION ACTIVITIES

Place the bottles, funnels, aprons and jugs outside next to the water tray and encourage the children to explore the range of sounds they can make as independently as possible during their play.

86. Which One Am I?

Learning Objective

Developing

Pupils respond to other pupils in music sessions.

Additional Skills

Social communication: playing a game as part of a small group.

Auditory: listening to and recognising familiar sounds.

Fine and gross motor: manipulating an instrument to make a sound.

Resources

A range of matching musical instruments

A screen (or instruments in a box and adult plays with their back to the group)

Symbol board with symbols of all the instruments (one per table)

MAIN

• To set up this activity place one set of the instruments on a table in the classroom. Place the symbol boards on three or four tables and place the matching set of instruments in a box or behind a screen.

• Support the children to come and sit at the tables, three to four children per table.

• Explain that they are going to listen to an instrument being played behind the screen and then must race to identify the instrument from the symbols. The first child to do this in the group can then run to the table of instruments, find the instrument and play it. The children are racing against their friends on the table and then their friends on the other tables.

• Keep a tally score of the table that is able to identify and then play the most instruments.

PLENARY

At the end of the lesson, reveal which table was able to identify and play the most instruments and support all the children to come to the instrument table, select their favourite instrument and play all together.

CONSOLIDATION ACTIVITIES

Repeat this lesson across the year as children become familiar with a wider range of instruments.

87. Indigenous Instruments

Learning Objective

Developing

Pupils explore the range of effects that can be made by an instrument.

Additional Skills

Attention: maintaining attention on an activity for up to 20 minutes.

Social communication: taking part in an imaginative activity within a group.

Fine motor and gross motor: manipulating an instrument to create a range of sounds.

Resources

Instruments indigenous to or originating from a chosen country, e.g. didgeridoo if exploring Australia, ukulele if exploring Hawaii

Pieces of music produced by the instruments

National anthem of chosen country

Pretend flight tickets to chosen country

Other props relating to that country including food

Hole punch

MAIN

• To set up this lesson, place the children's chairs in rows, as you would find in an aeroplane. In different areas of the classroom place the props and instruments relating to that country (Australia will be used in this example).

• Support the children to line up outside the classroom and explain that we are taking a trip to Australia! Give each child a flight ticket and ask a child to hole punch it as each child comes into the classroom and takes a seat on the 'aeroplane'.

• Pretend to take off and land in Australia. Play the national anthem of the country as children come off the 'plane'.

• Take children to the area of the classroom where the indigenous instruments are set up. Model using the different instruments to make sounds and then support all the children to take turns making a range of sounds with the didgeridoo, the gumleaf, etc.

• Record the children exploring the sounds they can make with the instruments.

PLENARY

Support the children to explore the other props and food whilst listening to the pieces of music made by the instruments; this could be professional recordings or the recordings of the children.

CONSOLIDATION ACTIVITIES

Repeat this activity and each week explore a different country and their indigenous instruments, e.g. Scotland and bagpipes, Hawaii and ukulele, etc.

Teaching note: if there are children in the class from different countries this lesson could be based on instruments from those countries and the children could possibly bring them in from home.

88. Historical Steps

Learning Objective

Developing

Pupils respond to others in a music lesson. Pupils move expressively in response to the music.

Additional Skills

Gross motor: coordinating movements to complete a dance routine.

Social communication: taking part in a group dance or routine.

Kinaesthetic: moving body appropriately in response to music.

Resources

A range of music (if possible with matching videos) from different eras that have dance routines associated with them such as 'The Barley Mow' from the 17th century, a Victorian dance such as the polka or quadrille, the Charleston from the 1920s, the Hustle from the 1970s, the Macarena from the 1990s, etc.

Photos or symbols to match the type of music

A large piece of paper with the types of music written across the top

A marker pen

Camera/electronic tablet

MAIN

• Support the children to sit with a view of the music/ videos of the music.

• Play the different music for the children and then take a vote on their favourite music. The piece with the most votes wins.

• Support the children to learn the dance associated with the music and to interact with each other as independently as possible as they respond to the music and learn the steps.

• Film the children performing their chosen dance once it has been learned.

PLENARY

Support the children to watch the recording of their dance and comment positively on each others' performances.

CONSOLIDATION ACTIVITIES

Repeat this activity and choose a different era and a different dance. Perform the children's favourite dance for a wider audience such as in an assembly or a school talent show.

89. Indigenous Tunes

Learning Objective

Developing

Pupils copy simple rhythms and musical patterns.

Additional Skills

Gross motor: using voice and body to imitate simple rhythms and musical patterns.

Auditory: listening and responding to a range of music using voice.

Social communication: taking part in an activity and responding to others in a small group.

Resources

Recordings of indigenous chanting and singing

Musical instruments that could be used to bang out simple rhythms, e.g. drums, rain sticks, etc.

Electronic tablet

MAIN

- Support the children to sit in a circle and to close their eyes. Play the recordings of the chanting and support the children to listen.

- Stop the music and ask the children to open their eyes. Explain that they are going to play the music again and this time the children are to join in using their voices.

- Support the children to do this by modelling joining in with the chanting and singing.

- Give the children the musical instruments and play the music again. This time everyone joins in using their voices and instruments to imitate the rhythm and musical patterns of the music.

- Record the children joining in with the singing and copying the rhythms and musical patterns of the music.

PLENARY

Support one child to come and sit in the middle of the circle and use their voice and instrument to create a rhythm or simple musical pattern. Encourage all the children to echo back the child's rhythm. The child then chooses a friend to come and replace them in the middle of the circle.

CONSOLIDATION ACTIVITIES

Listen to other music that has strong rhythmic and musical patterns using mostly voices and simple instruments and encourage the child to use their voice to imitate the rhythms and patterns that they hear.

90. Name That Tune

Learning Objective

Securing

Pupils create simple graphic scores using pictures.

Additional Skills

Auditory: listening to instructions.

Attention: building attention towards 20–25 minutes.

Fine motor: using scissors.

Resources

Print out of a grid of repeated musical instruments (row of drums, maracas, triangles, tambourines, etc.)

One large length of paper per child and one for adult to model

Scissors

Glue

MAIN

• Place out the printouts of the pictures of the musical instruments, glue and scissors.

• Invite the children to sit around the table. Model placing the paper down and looking at the page of instruments. Pick out an instrument, cut it out and place it on the paper. Repeat and talk through the process.

• Give each child a large length of paper (width just bigger than the pictures).

• Support the children where necessary but, if able, leave them to work as independently as possible.

PLENARY

Once everyone has finished, support each child to write their name on their score and give their song a title (if possible). Hand them to the adult and everyone helps tidy up.

CONSOLIDATION ACTIVITIES

As a follow on to this lesson, hand out the instruments and as a group, one by one, place the scores the children made on the board and everyone plays the song.

91. Follow My Lead

Learning Objective

Securing

Pupils communicate choices when playing.

Additional Skills

Auditory: listening to instructions.

Attention: building attention over 20 minutes.

Fine motor: using percussion instruments.

Social communication: following another child's lead.

Resources

Photocopies of the graphic scores from 'Name That Tune' lesson

Music stands

Instruments that correspond to the graphic scores

'Fast'/'slow'/'loud'/'quiet' visuals

MAIN

- Following on from the lesson 'Name That Tune', provide each child in the group with a photocopy of one of the graphic scores that were made; place these on the music stands (if available).

- The child whose score it is becomes the conductor; they hand out instruments to each group member. (Support by moving the children, so if three children have drums, they are all sat together.)

- The conductor is to set the tempo by showing either a fast or slow symbol and they point to the child(ren) in turn to play the instruments corresponding to the graphic score.

- Repeat with another child and their piece of music.

PLENARY

Everyone can have one last turn at playing their instruments with the adult instructing either fast, slow, loud or quiet. Then all the instruments get put away.

CONSOLIDATION ACTIVITIES

This lesson may have to go over a few lessons to ensure that each child has a turn at being the conductor.

92. Now This One I Like

Learning Objective

Securing

Pupils listen carefully to music.

Additional Skills

Auditory: listening to music.

Attention: building attention over 20 minutes.

Fine motor: mark making/writing.

Resources

Table handouts (as described in Main)

Five pre-selected pieces of music

Access to computer or electronic tablet to play music

Pencils

MAIN

• Provide each child with a handout that contains a table set out as follows: numbers 1–5 in the left-hand column, name of each song in the middle column and blank spaces in the right-hand columns.

• Inform the children that they are going to listen to five pieces of music. After each piece has been played twice, the children need to decide if they like it/don't like it (or, if able, articulate how it makes them feel) and this goes in the right-hand column with the corresponding number.

• Complete the first song together. Everyone sits at a table and has the sheet and pencil ready. Play the first piece of music twice. Ask another adult what they thought. Adult says if they liked it/did not like it and how it made them feel. Model finding number 1 in the table and following the boxes until the blank box is found and writing this in.

• Support the children to articulate their thoughts and complete the first box.

• Repeat with songs 2–5 with reduced adult support as the activity progresses.

PLENARY

Ask two of the children to share their thoughts: what was their favourite piece of music? Which, if any, didn't they like?

CONSOLIDATION ACTIVITIES

Create a voting system with smiley and sad faces either side of an A5 card. When a piece of music is played in class, ask the children to vote on it so they get used to making choices about different music they may or may not like.

93. Black and White Music

Learning Objective

Securing

Pupils make simple compositions.

Additional Skills

Visual: recognising colours.

Attention: maintaining attention on an activity for up to 20–25 minutes.

Fine motor: using a finger point to manipulate an instrument to make a sound.

Social communication: working as part of a pair.

Resources

Black and white colour symbols (several copies of each)

A3 paper

Glue sticks

A piano or keyboard (if none available use an app on an electronic tablet)

Camera/electronic tablet

MAIN

- Support each child to choose a friend to work with.

- Support the children to come to the piano/keyboard and explain there are 'black' and 'white' keys, supporting language with the colour symbols.

- Model making a simple musical score by sticking the black and white colour symbols in a line on a piece of A3 paper, e.g. 'black', 'black', 'white', 'black', 'white' and then following their score to play the black and white keys accordingly.

- Support each child to create their own score and then to conduct their friend to play their score on the piano/keyboard.

- Record the performance using the camera/electronic tablet.

PLENARY

Support the children to sit with a view of a screen so that they can watch back their performances of the simple sounds whilst they followed their friend's musical score. Support the children to comment on the music they made.

CONSOLIDATION ACTIVITIES

If possible, label the piano/keyboard keys with their correct notes, i.e. C, D, E, F, G, A, B, and then support the children to make musical scores for their friends to follow using the correct notes of the piano.

94. Bottle Orchestra Part 2

Learning Objective

Securing

Pupils follow simple graphic scores with symbols and play simple sequences of music.

Additional Skills

Social communication: taking turns as part of a small group.

Visual: responding to a visual cue to take a turn.

Fine and gross motor: manipulating an object to create a sound.

Resources

Aprons

Transparent, empty narrow neck bottles (glass or plastic)

Funnels

Water jugs

Camera/electronic tablet

Marker pen

1, 2, 3 number symbols (several copies of each and one set per group)

Interactive whiteboard (IWB)

MAIN

• Support the children to explore making different sounds with the bottles and water as in 'Bottle Orchestra Part 1'.

• Support the children in their small groups to decide on three bottles that make the best sound and label the bottles 1, 2 and 3.

• Support one child to be the 'conductor' by creating a 'musical score' by lining up the number symbols, e.g. 1, 1, 3, 2, 2, 1. The other children in the group pick up the bottles and follow the lead of the conductor to take part in the performance; adult films the performance.

• Repeat this so that all the children have a chance to be the conductor and the players in the orchestra.

PLENARY

At the end of the lesson support the children to carefully pour away all of the water and to come and sit with a view of the IWB. Lead adult shows the clips of the children's performances and supports them to comment on their musical performances.

CONSOLIDATION ACTIVITIES

Support the children to perform in their bottle orchestras for a larger audience, such as during a school assembly or talent show.

95. Musical Match

Learning Objective

Securing

Pupils listen to and describe music in simple terms.

Additional Skills

Attention: taking part in an activity for up to 25 minutes.

Social communication: taking part in a game within a larger group.

Communication: use speech or gesture to describe an idea to another person.

Resources

Laminated symbol bingo cards with simple musical terms, e.g. 'fast', 'slow', 'loud', 'quiet', 'high', 'low'

Whiteboard markers

A range of music that can be played through a CD player/interactive whiteboard that matches the musical terms

A musical instrument such as a shaker or drum

MAIN

- Support the children to come and sit at the table ready to learn.

- Explain that we are going to listen to music and identify how it is being played, e.g. loud or quiet, and then see if we have that word on our bingo boards.

- Model listening to a piece of music, identifying it as quiet and then looking at a bingo board to see if the term is there and then marking it off with an X.

- Give out the bingo boards and markers to the children and support them to listen to the music and identify how it is being played.

- The first child to mark off all their words is the winner!

- Swap around the bingo boards and play again.

PLENARY

Support the children to come and sit in a circle. Play the instrument in different ways and the children call out how it is being played, e.g. fast!

CONSOLIDATION ACTIVITIES

Across the day support the child to identify and describe sounds in simple terms, e.g. if a child is screaming as they play in the playground support the child to identify the sound as 'high'; if everyone is singing in assembly identify the sound as loud!

96. Play and Guess

Learning Objective

Securing

Pupils use a growing musical vocabulary of words, signs or symbols to describe what they hear, e.g. fast, slow, low, high, etc.

Additional Skills

Communication: responding to another child as part of a group using a growing vocabulary.

Auditory: listening to sounds and identifying how they are played.

Social communication: taking turns as part of a larger group.

Resources

Range of musical instruments that can be played in different ways, e.g. fast, slow, low, high, loudly and quietly (piano, xylophone, etc.)

Symbols to describe how the instrument is being played, e.g. 'loud', 'quiet', 'fast', 'slow', 'high', 'low' (several sets of these)

MAIN

• Support the children to come and sit in a circle.

• This lesson is played similar to charades; choose a child and show them a symbol of how an instrument can be played, e.g. loud, without showing it to anyone else. The child then selects an instrument from the range of musical instruments and plays it loudly.

• The other children in the group have to guess how the child is playing the instrument. The first child to guess correctly by calling out or showing the correct symbol swaps with the child playing the instrument and takes a turn being shown a different way an instrument can be played.

• Repeat this until all the children have had a turn.

PLENARY

Give all the children in the group an instrument; hold up the different symbols of how an instrument can be played and the children respond by trying to play their instrument in that way.

CONSOLIDATION ACTIVITIES

Support the children to play this game with an increasing vocabulary. This game could also be adapted so that the children have to guess what instrument the child is playing (they act it out or play it behind a screen) or a type of music (again the children act it out or play it from a selection on a computer).

97. Music Critic

Learning Objective

Securing

Pupils use a growing musical vocabulary of words, signs or symbols to describe what they hear, e.g. fast, slow, low, high, etc.

Additional Skills

Social communication: listening to a performance as part of a group.

Communication: using words, signs or symbols to express opinions and ideas to others.

Auditory: listening to live music.

Resources

Access to live music performance (either within the local community or a band to come into the school)

Any risk assessments needed in line with school trip policies

Symbols to support children to describe the music and express their views, e.g. 'loud', 'quiet', 'fast', 'slow', 'high', 'low', 'like', 'didn't like', instrument symbols, etc.

Glue sticks

Paper

MAIN

- Support the children to experience a live performance of music either out in the local community or invite a band or musician to come and play in the school.

- After the performance, support the children to discuss what they heard. Support children to use vocabulary that describes the type of music, e.g. jazz, classical, etc., the instruments used, were there loud and quiet parts? Was the pitch high or low? Was the music fast or slow?

- Also support the children to discuss the parts of the music they did and didn't like and to try and give reasons for their opinions.

PLENARY

Support the children to write a short review of the musical performance by writing words or making sentences using the symbols and glue. Encourage the children to share their reviews with another class or member of the senior leadership team.

CONSOLIDATION ACTIVITIES

Repeat this process for other musical performances given by other children in the school or class or listened to on the IWB.

98. Outside Chorus Part 1

Learning Objective

Securing

Pupils create their own simple compositions, carefully selecting sounds.

Additional Skills

Fine motor: using equipment such as sound recorder/ electronic tablet/ computer mouse to make and compile composition.

Auditory: listening for sounds in the environment.

Communication: communicating choices, ideas and experiences to another person.

Resources

Sound recorder/ electronic tablet

Symbols to match sounds heard outside, e.g. 'birds', 'siren', 'voices', 'car', 'beeping', etc.

Sounds sheet (A4 paper with 'Sounds Sheet' title, one per child)

MAIN

- Explain that the children are going to make their own piece of music using sounds they hear outside. The children are going to go outside and use the sound recorder/tablet to record different sounds that they hear and then make them into a piece of music.

- Support the children to go outside, identify individual sounds, e.g. birds, car beeping, etc., and to record a sound bite of those sounds.

- Back in the classroom support the children to listen to their sound bites and identify the different sounds using the symbols.

- Support the children to select their favourite sounds from the sound bites by selecting the symbols and sticking them on their 'Sounds Sheet'.

PLENARY

Support the children to come together and take it in turns to discuss the sounds they heard and recorded and share their favourite sounds with the group.

CONSOLIDATION ACTIVITIES

Encourage the children to listen carefully to sounds in their environment and see if they can identify them by labelling them and also identify how they sound, e.g. loud, high, etc.

99. Outside Chorus Part 2

Learning Objective

Securing

Pupils create their own simple compositions, carefully selecting sounds.

Additional Skills

Fine motor: using equipment such as sound recorder/electronic tablet/computer mouse to make and compile composition.

Communication: communicating choices, ideas and experiences to another person.

Attention: recalling skills and activities from a previous lesson.

Resources

The child's 'Sounds Sheets' from 'Outside Chorus Part 1'

Several copies of the symbols of the sounds each child chose

A3 paper

Glue sticks

Access to a simple playback method of the child's chosen sound bites, e.g. a computer file with the sounds, a simple music editing app, the sounds lined up on a sound recorder

MAIN

• Support the children to remind themselves of the sound bites that they chose from the previous lesson by looking at their 'Sounds Sheets' and listening to their sound bites.

• Model for the class making a simple composition by selecting a sound symbol, e.g. 'bird', sticking it on the A3 paper using the glue stick and then selecting another sound, e.g. 'siren', and sticking that next to it, continuing until they have made a short composition by selecting the outside sounds and placing them in their preferred order.

• Then model playing back the sound bites in the order that they have been compiled. This could be recorded again, or if it is being done in a simple music-editing app then the piece has been put together.

• Support the children to make their compositions using the symbols of the carefully chosen outside sounds and then playing and recording the sound bites to develop their piece of music.

PLENARY

Once the children have completed their piece of music compiled from the outside sounds, support them to play their pieces for the rest of the class. Support the children to comment on the music using their developing musical vocabulary, e.g. 'That part was quiet.' 'The siren sound was high.'

CONSOLIDATION ACTIVITIES

Support children to place symbols or pictures of instruments in a line and then play them in that order during their free playtime.

100. Drum Circle

Learning Objective

Securing

Pupils listen to and contribute to sound stories and are involved in simple improvisations.

Additional Skills

Auditory: listening and responding to their name.

Social communication: taking turns as part of a larger group.

Gross motor: controlling movements to create a rhythm.

Resources

A drum per child

Electronic tablet/video camera

Interactive whiteboard (IWB)

MAIN

- Support the children to come and sit in a circle and give each child a drum.

- Explain that we are going to make a 'drum story' with everybody adding a sentence by making a rhythm.

- Model a simple, short drumming rhythm and then say another adult's name; they repeat the first adult's rhythm and add their own and then say another name to pass the rhythm on.

- Support the children to join in to build up an increasingly lengthy drumming session made up of different rhythms.

- Adult films the session.

- Repeat this several times to make different drumming stories.

PLENARY

Once all the children have joined in and the activity has been filmed, support the children to sit with a view of the IWB. Play back the recording of the drum circle and support the children to comment on their rhythms, e.g. fast, slow, loud, quiet, etc.

CONSOLIDATION ACTIVITIES

Repeat this activity using different instruments.

101. Classroom Conductor

Learning Objective

Securing

Pupils make and communicate choices when composing.

Additional Skills

Social communication: sharing and communicating ideas to a larger group.

Communication: making choices from photos and symbols.

Auditory: beginning to select sounds that match tempo and pitch of a piece of music.

Resources

Symbols/photos to match the instruments (several copies of each)

Range of instruments

Pictures of the children in the class or group

A selection of familiar music for the child to choose from (could be nursery rhymes, classical music, recent music)

A conductor's baton!

MAIN

- Support each child to select a familiar piece of music from a small range of symbols/photos/sounds.

- Then work with the child to listen to the music and select instruments that best match the music at different points, e.g. if 'Twinkle Twinkle Little Star' has been chosen, maybe a triangle for the words 'twinkle' would work well.

- Support the child to lay out all the symbols/photos of the chosen instruments and then to select the children's photos to match to the instruments to decide who will play each instrument in their performance. The child may choose to have more than one member of the class/group play a certain instrument, e.g. if 'Jingle Bells' is the chosen song, the child might want three children playing bells.

- Then support the child to organise the class/group into an 'orchestra' by instructing them to sit in certain places with the instruments they are going to play.

- Play the chosen piece of music and the child acts as conductor, indicating to the children in the orchestra when to play their instruments.

- Adult films the performance.

PLENARY

Play the performance back to the child (possibly along with the rest of the group/class) and encourage them to comment on their choices, e.g. Was the triangle a good choice? Were three people playing the bells good?

CONSOLIDATION ACTIVITIES

Support the child to work with a partner to repeat this lesson but this time choosing a different piece of music and communicating their ideas and choices as independently as possible to their partner.

Kate Bradley had a background in occupational therapy before re-training as a teacher. She has worked in both mainstream and special needs schools, making lessons fun and engaging for SEN learners. Kate holds a Masters in Special and Inclusive Education, and lives in London.

Claire Brewer has been teaching pupils with severe learning difficulties, profound and multiple learning difficulties and autism since completing her PGCE at Goldsmiths University. Claire holds a Masters in Special and Inclusive Education, and lives in London.

Also by Kate Bradley and Claire Brewer

101 Inclusive and SEN Maths Lessons
Fun Activities and Lesson Plans for Children Aged 3–11

136 pages
Paperback
ISBN 978 1 78592 101 8

Create an inclusive classroom for all through engaging maths activities such as Shape Bingo, Cake Splat! and Fruity Fractions, all of which have been matched to the UK National Curriculum P Levels 4–8. Tailored to the specific P Level, each lesson plan includes a learning objective, the resources needed, the main activity, a plenary and a consolidation activity to help support children's understanding.

When working with children, and especially those with SEN, lessons need to meet their interests as well as their needs by containing visual stimulus, movement and fine and gross motor skills, and the activities in this book have been specifically designed with this in mind. This straightforward and practical book offers you 101 creative classroom activities for teaching maths to pupils who are achieving at P Levels 4–8 and Key Stage One as well as mapping the range of additional skills they will acquire.

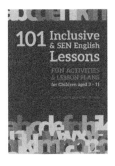

101 Inclusive and SEN English Lessons
Fun Activities and Lesson Plans for
Children Aged 3–11

160 pages
Paperback
ISBN 978 1 78592 365 4

Create an inclusive classroom for all with this resource, full of ideas for engaging and accessible English lessons. Each lesson is tailored to objectives for children working below National Curriculum levels and includes a learning objective, the resources needed, the main activity, a plenary and a consolidation activity to help support children's understanding.

When working with children, and especially those with SEN, lessons need to meet their interests as well as their needs by containing visual stimulus and promoting fine and gross motor skills, and the activities in this book have been specifically designed with this in mind. This straightforward and practical book offers you 101 creative classroom activities for teaching English to pupils who are achieving at P Levels 4–8, as well as mapping the range of additional skills they will acquire.

101 Inclusive and SEN Science and Computing Lessons
Fun Activities and Lesson Plans for Children Aged 3–11

152 pages
Paperback
ISBN 978 1 78592 366 1

Create an inclusive classroom with these fun and accessible activities for science and computing lessons. Each lesson is tailored to objectives for children working below National Curriculum levels and includes a learning objective, the resources needed, the main activity, a plenary and a consolidation activity to support children's understanding and engagement.

When working with children, and especially those with SEN, lessons need to meet their interests as well as their needs by containing visual stimulus and promoting fine and gross motor skills. The activities in this book have been specifically designed with this in mind. Straightforward and practical, it offers 101 creative classroom activities for teaching Science and Computing to pupils who are working below national curriculum levels, as well as mapping the range of additional skills they will acquire.

101 Inclusive and SEN Humanities and Language Lessons
Fun Activities and Lesson Plans for Children Aged 3–11

144 pages
Paperback
ISBN 978 1 78592 367 8

Create an inclusive classroom for all with this resource. From Sensory Box Fire Station to Victorian Me, this book is overflowing with ideas for engaging and accessible geography, history and language lessons. Each lesson is tailored for children working below National Curriculum levels and includes a learning objective, the resources needed, the main activity, a plenary and a consolidation activity to help support children's understanding.

The activities in this book have been specifically designed to promote fine and gross motor skills and utilise lots of visual stimulus, which is important for working with children with SEN. This straightforward and practical book offers you 101 creative classroom activities for teaching humanities and languages to pupils who are working below national curriculum levels, as well as mapping the range of additional skills they will acquire.

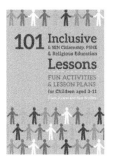

101 Inclusive and SEN Citizenship, PSHE and Religious Education Lessons
Fun Activities and Lesson Plans for Children Aged 3–11

144 pages
Paperback
ISBN 978 1 78592 368 5

Create an inclusive classroom for all with these fun and accessible activities for PSHE, Citizenship and Religious Education lessons. Each lesson is tailored for children working below National Curriculum levels and includes a learning objective, the resources needed, the main activity, a plenary and a consolidation activity to help support children's understanding. These subjects are key to teaching children the concepts of self-awareness, independence and community, which can be difficult to teach to children with SEN but are vital for their self-esteem and mental wellbeing.

The activities in this book have been specifically designed to promote fine and gross motor skills and utilise lots of visual stimulus, which is important for working with children with SEN. This straightforward and practical book offers you 101 creative classroom activities for teaching Citizenship, PSHE and Religious Education to pupils who are working below national curriculum levels, as well as mapping the range of additional skills they will acquire.

CPI Antony Rowe
Eastbourne, UK
September 28, 2024